of passersby—major Western government institutions—who had the where-withal to help but did not, and of a few smaller Western organizations who did stop to help but could not provide enough to prevent massive flight. In the end, it is an exhortation to the rest of us would-be Samaritans to wake up and respond to the suffering of these and all survivors of harsh denials of their religious freedom."

—Daniel Philpott, Professor of Political Science,
University of Notre Dame

"*The Disappearing People* provides a vivid account of an entire religious community's near-extinction in the very place of its birth, the ancient Middle East, at the hands of Islamist extremists. By implication, author Stephen Rasche has also described an existential threat that confronts all of us, Muslim and non-Muslim alike. It simply remains to be seen whether we will heed his warning and act in time to prevent similar disasters from befalling those of us who dwell in blessed lands, seemingly distant from the horrifying chaos that engulfs so much of the Islamic world."

—KH. Yahya Cholil Staquf, General Secretary of Nahdlatul Ulama, the world's largest Muslim Organization, and Cofounder of the Global Humanitarian Islam Movement

THE
DISAPPEARING
PEOPLE

THE TRAGIC FATE
OF CHRISTIANS
IN THE MIDDLE EAST

STEPHEN M. RASCHE

BOMBARDIER
BOOKS

A BOMBARDIER BOOKS BOOK
An Imprint of Post Hill Press

The Disappearing People:
The Tragic Fate of Christians in the Middle East
© 2020 by Stephen M. Rasche
All Rights Reserved

ISBN: 978-1-64293-203-4
ISBN (eBook): 978-1-64293-204-1

Interior design and composition by Greg Johnson, Textbook Perfect

This is a work of nonfiction. All people, locations, events, and situations are portrayed to the best of the author's memory.

Post Hill Press
New York • Nashville
posthillpress.com

Published in the United States of America

To my Grandfather
Dr. Robert L. Rasche, ThD.

CONTENTS

Until this hour we are hungry and we are thirsty, we are naked, we are abused, and we have no dwelling place, And we toil as we labor with our hands. They dishonor us and we bless; they persecute us and we endure. They accuse us and we beg them. We are as the scum of the world and the offscouring of every person until now.

1 Corinthians 4:11–13
(Translation from Aramaic Bible)

Foreword

Over the past two decades, terrorists and sectarians have shredded the rich multi-religious and ethnic tapestry of Iraq. Violent Islamist extremists have driven the Christians and Yazidis from their homes with genocide, crimes against humanity, and war crimes. The Christian minority is now on the verge of extinction in their historic homeland.

Christians have been in Iraq since the very birth of the church. Some who were persecuted in Rome at the beginning of the Christian era even took refuge in what is now Erbil, in northern Iraq.

There were between 1.3 and 1.5 million Christians in Iraq before the US invasion in 2003. Taking advantage of the chaos that ensued, sectarians persecuted the Christians from the start of that ill-fated intervention. It was bad for religious and ethnic minorities under Hussein, but it has been immeasurably worse in the aftermath. The Christian population had been driven down to 500,000 before ISIS began its genocidal campaign. Now just a small remnant remains.

The current tragedy has transpired against the backdrop of a centuries-old persecution of minorities combined with the ever-simmering sectarian conflict between Sunni and Shia Muslims. A tenacious Sunni minority dominated modern Iraq since the 1920s, and the dictator Saddam Hussein suppressed the Shia especially brutally. When the United States unseated Saddam, the tables were turned in favor of the Shia. Sectarian tension turned even more violent when Sunni Al-Qaeda in Iraq blew up the al-Askari Shrine, one of the holiest sites for Shia, in Samarra in February 2006. Religious and ethnic minorities, already subject to a long history of attacks, were caught between the combatants and targeted further.

When ISIS savagely drove Christians from their Mosul and Nineveh homelands in the summer of 2014, over 100,000 of them sought refuge in the semi-autonomous Kurdistan Region of Iraq. Most of these ended up in Erbil, the Kurdish capital, where it fell to the Chaldean Catholic Archdiocese of Erbil, under the leadership of Archbishop Bashar Warda, to provide food, shelter, and medicine to Chaldean and Syriac Catholics; Orthodox, Assyrian, and Armenian Christians; as well as to scattered groups of Yazidis and Muslims who sought help from Erbil's Christian community.

The fate of Iraqi religious and ethnic minorities has also rested, in part, in other hands: the United Nations, the United States Agency for International Development (USAID) and State Department, other bilateral assistance programs, and a host of non-governmental relief agencies and church entities. As this book painfully describes, the global response has often been woefully inadequate.

In these agonizing years, what has it been like to be an internally displaced Christian in Iraq? What has it been like to be a bishop, priest, or layperson responsible for caring for internally displaced people (IDPs)? Stephen Rasche's book searingly answers these questions.

Rasche is an American lawyer who had been working on projects in Iraq since 2007. In the wake of the ISIS attacks in 2014, his friend Archbishop Warda upended his life by asking him to remain in Erbil to provide full-time counsel and help to Christians and other genocide survivors in the care of the bishop. After what was admittedly a difficult reflection, Rasche accepted this challenging assignment. Since then, he has coordinated assistance to the IDPs and served as their main point of contact with governments, the United Nations, aid groups, journalists, diaspora organizations, and other entities around the world, shuttling between Iraq, the United States, and Europe.

Rasche has been in the trenches with the embattled minorities, including living months at a time out in the disputed lands where the displaced hoped somehow to return. There is perhaps no more informed western witness to the plight of the survivors and to the scandal of the world's disjointed efforts to help them.

The Disappearing People is not a history book. It is a poignant series of painful vignettes about unfulfilled promises, bureaucratic cul-de-sacs, and inefficient, ineffective, and expensive United Nations assistance programs. It shows the heartbreaking impact of foreign governments' refusal to provide effective help for the displaced minorities to remain in their ancestral homelands, and their particular and puzzling aversion to funding the faith-based entities dedicated to serving genocide survivors on the ground. And it chronicles the complicity of the government of Iraq and the international community in the Iran-backed militias' attempted colonization of Christian and Yazidi villages on the Nineveh Plains, or at least, their ineptness in countering this colonization.

As a former senior official at USAID and a former executive at World Vision, I am quite familiar with the real difficulties of working in and with government bureaucracies, and I am fully aware of the rationales given to justify inaction. I also know that much good has and is being done by international and national aid agencies, including USAID, and there are dedicated public servants here who have tried to do their best to make a difference. But nevertheless, there is no denying three indisputable facts:

First, Christians are on the verge of disappearing from Iraq and other countries in the Middle East. We have simply failed to stop the bleeding. Without the timely, sacrificial support of Aid to the Church in Need, the Knights of Columbus, and the government of Hungary, who all stepped in early on when American and other international assistance was not reaching the internally displaced Christians, the situation would have been immeasurably worse.

Second, all of our rhetoric and promises have rarely resulted in effective, timely programming. When help has arrived—if at all—it has often come after the IDPs' opportunity to return home has been lost or significantly reduced. Illustrative of the problem is USAID's initial, disastrous failure to faithfully implement Vice President Mike Pence's promise on October 26, 2017, that assistance would flow "directly" to religious minorities in Iraq. Not until two years later, in early October 2019, did USAID finally announce the first of such "direct assistance" awards—six grants totaling $4 million, including $710,000 to the Catholic University of Erbil (founded and supported by the Chaldean Archdiocese of Erbil) to provide classes in basic business and employment skills for the victims of genocide. USAID Administrator Mark Green on October 3, 2019, frankly acknowledged in the following tweet that no direct awards to ethnic and religious minorities in Iraq had, in fact, occurred in over a decade and a half.

> *USAID's New Partnership Initiative helps us engage with new, local partners. In Iraq, this allows us to partner directly with local orga-nizations for the first time in 16 years, helping ethnic and religious minority communities rebuild after ISIS genocide.*[1]

About the same time, USAID announced a $6.8 million grant to the NGO Catholic Relief Services (a long-time USAID partner globally). A portion of this grant was to provide food vouchers for displaced persons in Erbil (Christians and Yazidis—including many whom the Chaldean Archdiocese of Erbil had struggled for five years to care for with no US government or UN support). USAID also announced awards of $9 million each to its long-time partner, the UN's International Organi-zation of Migration (IOM), and the evangelical relief NGO Samaritan's Purse (another long-time USAID global partner) for "the return and recovery of displaced religious and ethnic minorities."

Much good can come from this programming, it is hoped; **the problem is that 90 percent of the Christians have already fled the country**—many during the previous five years when we had failed to respond quickly and in a way which targeted the IDPs where they actually were and with what they most needed. Ignoring the repeated specific requests, nearly all of them modest and eminently practical, from the IDPs and their representatives, aid agencies, including the UN and USAID, instead pro-duced their own sets of priorities and forced all aid assistance through their own paradigms. The result has been a questionable use of enor-mous amounts of funding, and, most tragically, an ongoing failure to substantively change the trajectory of survival for the displaced Chris-tians and Yazidis themselves.

The US government claims to have spent more than $340 million since the vice president's October 2017 policy statement on supporting

---

[1] Green, Mark. Twitter Post. October 3, 2019, 9:22 AM. https://twitter.com/usaid markgreen/status/1179793751193067523?s=21.

religious and ethnic minorities in Iraq. But the main measure of success has seemed to be whether money was spent and how much, not whether aid has effectively stemmed the exodus of these genocide survivors out of Iraq. Funds have mainly gone for large infrastructure projects in the Nineveh Plains, even though this region has been mainly depopulated of religious and ethnic minorities.

Meanwhile, many of the displaced minorities have been unable to return to their homelands for security reasons, because their houses are still in shambles (a need USAID said it could not address), or because the decimated local economy does not allow them to support their families. Yet until late 2019, the US government had failed to authorize monies to help these IDPs maintain survivability in the areas outside Nineveh (namely Erbil but also in other enclaves throughout Iraq) where most of them had been forced to flee and have been living, thus increasing the pressure on them to leave Iraq entirely.

For Western decision makers and aid organizations, arguing about the reasons we have failed to move quickly or effectively in the past five years does not get us very far and is not a good use of time. At the end of the day, the vast majority of the Christians and other minorities have already disappeared while we failed to respond in a way which could stem the outflow.

The point of Rasche's book is to take us inside the Christian community and, to an extent, the Yazidi community as well—into their uncertainty and fears, concrete needs, hopes, deep frustrations, and agonizing decisions of whether to stay or give up on Iraq and simply leave. It is a moving insight into what it is like to be part of a "disappearing people" who often have been forgotten and abandoned.

Third, beyond the inadequacies of bureaucratic assistance delivery, US national security policy and USAID failed to grasp fully the critical importance of protecting pluralism and the rights and needs of all religious and ethnic minorities, including Christians. The empirical evidence overwhelmingly affirms that protecting the presence of multi-ethnic and multi-religious communities is a powerful indicator of what leads to peace and stability. Nilay Saiya's *Weapon of Peace: How Religious Liberty Combats Terrorism* provides compelling, empirical evidence that this, in fact, is the case.

Religious freedom is essential to our national security. That is why Democratic and Republican presidents have included support for religious freedom in every National Security Strategy of the United States since 1997 (the first NSS to refer to it), with 2010 as the only exception. It therefore follows that a programmatic commitment to religious freedom should be part of our disaster assistance response.

Following conflicts in which people are targeted and displaced because of their faith, there is a very limited window of time to help the displaced return to their homes—a window that will rapidly close if we do not move with urgency. We ought to prioritize assistance that enables religious and ethnic minorities to survive and thrive, not just because it is "right" to help survivors but because it is prudent. These are not niche matters that the State Department or USAID can attend to after the "big" issues are resolved or when sufficient pressure arises from the outside to compel the US government to help.

If we really understood that it is essential for religious and ethnic minorities to survive as a matter of national and regional security, then momentum would be generated, which would sweep away the bureaucratic maneuvering, political infighting and delays that bogged down the delivery of effective and timely assistance to religious and ethnic minorities in Iraq these last five years.

The Office of Foreign and Disaster Assistance at USAID has a much-deserved reputation for being able to move quickly and efficiently when lives hang in the balance after a natural catastrophe. But when it comes to the survival of genocide-targeted communities in Iraq, USAID as a whole has lacked that same sense of priority or urgency. In the critical period following the defeat of ISIS, the UN and USAID prioritized returning IDPs to Mosul, most of whom were Muslim, rather than insisting that *both* majority and minority groups would be assisted. A considerably higher percentage of non-minorities returned to their homes than minorities, and as a result, minority homes and lands slipped into other hands, with very little chance of ever returning to their original owners.

While Rasche's book allows the reader to incarnate the harrowing, on-the-ground realities of these three facts, it is not just an interesting period piece about the plight of disappearing Christian and Yazidi minorities in Iraq. It is a book that compels us to learn from our failures as we continue to partner with Christians and Yazidis holding on in Iraq, and, one would hope, will empower our policies and programming relative to minorities elsewhere in the world in dire need of focused and effective assistance.

On the basis of what we have learned, we ought to do the following in Iraq:

First, the Christian population in Iraq may be down 90 percent, but that is no excuse to avoid effectively supporting those who remain and other displaced minorities where they are currently. Economic assistance programs ought to ensure that their needs are met and that they can sustain themselves in northern Iraq and in the remaining enclaves in the south. Our policy needs to be agile and inclusive enough to pivot between rebuilding the Nineveh Plains, the homeland to which many Christian IDPs still hope to return, and other areas, including the city of Erbil, where many remaining IDPs currently live. There are promising signs at the end of 2019 that USAID is beginning to do more directly with and for the IDPs where they actually are. These efforts must continue.

Second, we ought to have serious programming to help religious and ethnic minority refugees stranded in Jordan, Turkey, and Lebanon. If Iraq can stabilize, then we ought to help these refugees return to Iraq where possible, and do so safely, voluntarily, and with dignity. If Iraq does not stabilize in the near or medium term, we ought to help them resettle somewhere else in the world, including in the United States. The plight of these refugees bears the clear fingerprints of US foreign policy decisions made by both political parties—decisions for which the refugees themselves are wholly innocent. Summoning the political courage to address this honestly should not lie beyond us.

Third, we must ensure that the administration issues written policy directives which make it clear that US foreign assistance can and should prioritize direct investments in indigenous Iraqi entities, including faith-based entities. Throughout the crisis, there has been no US law or USAID and State Department rule or regulation prohibiting this kind of partnering. But because of ongoing bureaucratic intransigence or resistance, Congress unanimously passed the bipartisan Iraq and Syria

Genocide Relief and Accountability Act, authored by Rep. Chris Smith (R) and lead cosponsored by Rep. Anna Eshoo (D), which clearly authorizes such assistance. President Donald Trump signed it into law on December 11, 2018, at an Oval Office ceremony.

During my time with USAID, we provided assistance directly through a wide variety of faith-based organizations, including indigenous religious ones, with PEPFAR (the President's Emergency Plan for AIDS Relief) as part of the successful global fight against HIV/AIDS. The initial tranche of USAID New Partners Initiative grants in Iraq announced in October 2019 indicated a growing willingness to replicate best practices from PEPFAR, and such initiatives should be continued and expanded.

However, there are unquestionably those within the bureaucracy who presume indigenous entities are unable to capably deliver assistance, despite compelling facts to the contrary. Worse, some of these same bureaucrats believe that it is unconstitutional and discriminatory to assist entities—especially indigenous faith-based ones—where the intention is to specifically help minority religious and ethnic communities facing persecution. They hold this position even to the point of ignoring US law.

Their view overlooks the uncontestable fact that small genocide-targeted minorities are uniquely at-risk, while larger religious and ethnic communities face no such existential threat. The purpose of directed assistance is to enable these communities to survive, not unjust favoritism.

Legal and procurement guidelines must be written and enforced to make it clear that it is in our national interest for US foreign assistance programs to partner with faith-based entities where justified, including indigenous ones.

Fourth, we need to ensure that US national security policy—including federal budgets, USAID and State Department policies, rules, regulations, and funding decisions—fully and explicitly prioritize protecting religious freedom and the survival of religious and ethnic minorities in troubled regions of the world. It is wonderful and indeed consistent with our highest ideals as a country if we defend and assist ethnic and religious minorities because we care deeply for those who suffer. But it is also critical to understand that promoting religious freedom and enabling religious and ethnic minorities to survive and thrive is really in our own national security best interests and key to a healthy, stable, and peaceful world.

I would like to conclude with the words of Chaldean Catholic Bishop of Aleppo Antoine Audo, for they remind us of why Christians and other minorities matter.

> *It's important for us as Christians to be alive in the original lands of our fathers in the Middle East. Not only for us but for the church in the world...We have a long history of living together with Muslim people....it is very important to have Christian-Arab presence. If we lose it, I am convinced it will be a big loss for Islam, too.*[2]

KENT R. HILL is Senior Fellow for Eurasia, Middle East and Islam at the Religious Freedom Institute in Washington, DC. He is a former acting Administrator at USAID, where he also served as Assistant Administrator for the Bureau of Global Health and Assistant Administrator for the Bureau for Europe and Eurasia. Hill served as Senior Vice President of International Programs for World Vision and as Vice President of Character Development at the Templeton Foundation. Hill holds a PhD in Russian History from the University of Washington and, from 1992 to 2001, served as President of Eastern Nazarene College.

---

[2] Cited in Mindy Belz, *They Say We Are Infidels: On the Run from ISIS with Persecuted Christians in the Middle East* (Carol Stream, IL: Tyndale, 2016), 202-03.

Introduction

A word on how I ended up in the position to write this book:

I had been living in the midst of the ISIS war in Iraq for over three years when I decided to begin writing this book. I had been encouraged to do so on many occasions by people who heard myself and others speak about what was taking place in Iraq. While the scenes of ISIS terror were known in a general sense to most in the US, the specific realities of the displacement and suffering of the minorities, including Christians, was something that was far less clearly understood, and that the ancient Christian communities were now on the brink of extinction was something barely understood at all.[3] Although it was becoming increasingly clear that the story needed to be told to a broader audience, I remained hesitant for two reasons.

First, as a matter of practical reality, I was concerned for my safety. I was a member of the staff of the Chaldean Catholic Archdiocese of Erbil. I held a brief with significant responsibilities in the stabilization and restoration of the Christian towns in Nineveh, as they were slowly freed from the grip of ISIS. During this time, I lived with and among the priests and people of these ancient communities. My ability to

---

[3] The Christians of Iraq are primarily comprised of Chaldeans, Syriacs, Armenians, and Assyrians, with Chaldeans representing approximately 80 percent of the total population. The majority of Iraqi Christians are Eastern Rite Catholics in communion with the Holy See in Rome, with smaller numbers of Orthodox. Within the Chaldean, Syriac, and Assyrian populations, many still speak in dialects of Aramaic, the language of Jesus Christ. Christianity is believed to have come to Iraq through the first apostles in the first century A.D. In recent years, a small Protestant community has arrived primarily through American missionaries.

move about in the country, and be effective, lay in large measure to the low-profile manner I had adopted over many years of working in the region. To speak in front of a small group of think tank experts in Washington, DC, or testify as a witness at a low-visibility government hearing in the West, was one thing. To invite the kind of attention that came from writing a book and to speak about it in the broader media was quite another. I still had a lot of work left to do and telling the truth of what had actually taken place would, in some cases, mean going through a one-way door, one that I might not be able to go back through again.

Second, there was no clear end in sight for the Christians of Iraq. The aid that finally started to come was often misplaced and thwarted by corruption and outside politics. Security in the recovered towns remained tenuous, with new bands of oppressors taking the place of ISIS. ISIS itself was going underground, but it was not going away into history. "They shaved their beards," said one Iraqi Christian priest to me as we drove through the former ISIS stronghold of Telkayf, "but not their brains."

So why then did I decide to write this book now? In the simplest terms, because the sand has nearly run out in the hourglass that is Christianity in Iraq. Many of the other Christian communities of the Middle East are not far behind. And although there is still time left for small remnants of hope, if they are not acted upon now, this history of two thousand years will see its final chapters in our lifetimes—much of it perhaps even within this coming decade. But if any responsive, effective plan of action is to have purpose, it will need to be based in new thinking, which admits the reality of the situation, unclouded by Western aspirational paradigms, and the knee-jerk tendency to resort to claims of phobias and bias, which serve only to obscure truth.

There were, within living memory, over 1.3 million Christians in Iraq. There are, by most reliable counts, fewer than 150,000 today.[4] That is truth, and none of it happened naturally. It happened because of human-imposed conduct and policy, which had direct and foreseeable, even intended, consequences. A proper introduction to the situation we

---

[4] U.S. Department of State, Bureau of Democracy, Human Rights and Labor, *Iraq 2018 Religious Freedom Report*. Accessed October 2019. https://www.state.gov/wp-content/uploads/2019/05/IRAQ-2018-INTERNATIONAL-RELIGIOUS-FREEDOM-REPORT.pdf.

faced can be found in these excerpts of testimony below from myself and the courageous Yazidi survivor, Ms. Shireen, during our first testimony before Congress in 2016.[5]

STEPHEN M. RASCHE, ESQ., LEGAL COUNSEL AND DIRECTOR OF IDP RESETTLEMENT PROGRAMS, CHALDEAN CATHOLIC ARCHDIOCESE OF ERBIL, KURDISTAN REGION, IRAQ

Mr. RASCHE. Thank you, Mr. Chairman and distinguished members of the Commission, for allowing me to speak to you today on behalf of the persecuted Christians of Northern Iraq, who as of today number barely 200,000, down from over 1.5 million just 13 years ago.

Again, my name is Stephen Rasche and I serve on the staff of the Chaldean Catholic Archdiocese of Erbil in the Kurdistan region of Northern Iraq. And my intention here this morning is to give you a brief overview of the work we're doing and address our future needs and concerns.

At present, we at the archdiocese are serving the various needs of approximately 10,500 displaced families—IDPs in our language. The majority of these were originally Christian residents of Mosul and the Nineveh Plain. Within this overall number, nearly 6,000 families are presently receiving housing rental assistance at a total cost of approximately $650,000 per month. Our food package program serves over 10,000 families at a cost of approximately $720,000 per month, and our medical clinics serve over 6,000 families per month, at a total cost of about $80,000 per month, inclusive of all medicines.

While our responsibility at the archdiocese lies primarily with service to the Christian IDPs, we have regularly extended care to non-Christians as well. We do that as part of our mission. Our schools and medical clinics serve the Yazidis and Muslim IDPs, and our food and housing rental programs include many Yazidi families.

---

[5] See: Commission on Security and Cooperation in Europe, *Atrocities in Iraq and Syria: Relief for Survivors and Accountability for Perpetrators*, September 22, 2016. Accessed October 2019. https://www.csce.gov/international-impact/events/atrocities-iraq-syria-relief -survivors-and-accountability-perpetrators.

All of this work has been done using, exclusively, private aid, which today totals approximately $26 million since the outset of the recent crisis beginning in August of 2014. Our largest donors include the European-based Aid to the Church in Need, the Knights of Columbus, the U.S.-based Nazarene Fund, the Italian Episcopal Conference, the Chaldean Churches of the USA, and Caritas of Italy.

Members of this Commission, it is no exaggeration to say that without these private donors, the situation for Christians in Northern Iraq would have already collapsed and the vast majority of these families would, without question, have already joined the refugee diaspora now destabilizing the Middle East and Europe.

I say this because, throughout this entire period of crisis, other than initial supplies of tents and tarps, the Christian community in Iraq has received no funding from any U.S. aid agencies or the U.N. The reason for this, we are told repeatedly, lies in the Individual Needs Policy rigidly—in the present case, we would argue, blindly— adhered to by the U.S. Government and the U.N., as well as other U.S.-backed aid agencies.

Specifically, when we've approached any of these agencies regarding the provision of aid funding to the Christians, we've been told that we've done too well in our private efforts, and that the standards we've provided for our people exceed the minimum Individual Needs standards currently within the capabilities of those agencies. Counterarguments from us that the needs of our perishing population require a different standard of evaluation are met with vague sympathy but little else.

With all this as background—and as the time of forced displacement is now over two years—our private donors are running out of the ability to sustain our current level of care. And this brings us to two critical points to share with this Commission this morning.

First, while the standard of care being received by Christians may, in fact, marginally exceed that being provided elsewhere by the U.N. and similar organizations, there are no other groups in Iraq that are facing the existential threat now being faced by the Christians. This enhanced level of care is critical if we are to keep the Christian community viable in Iraq.

Secondly, from a moral standpoint, the uniquely endangered status of the Christian population, in our view, requires that they be viewed not as individuals, using the standard Individual Needs assessment, but rather as a group threatened with extinction as a people, the victims of genocide and historical violence which seeks to remove them permanently from their ancestral homes.

In response to a follow-up question from the chair:

Mr. RASCHE. Yes, Mr. Chairman. As I said in my written testimony, the needs that we are meeting are fundamental daily needs: shelter, food, medicine. They're not the type of needs that allow for us to tell people, "Hold on, it's coming in 6 months or 8 months or 12 months." They're at our door every morning, and our situation is one where we say, "We wake up every morning and we rob 6 Peters to pay 12 Pauls." We do that every day and we've been doing it every day for two years.

We are responsible for these people, and in the absence of government aid, we won't stop taking care of them. We will do what we need to do to find that aid wherever we need to find it.

The people, especially the Christians of the Kurdistan region in northern Iraq, view the Americans at present as their natural partners, and in all frankness, believe that the U.S. has a special moral role to play in this rebuilding.

But it is a real issue for us in that our donors are experiencing donor fatigue on their end. There's only so long that you can be asking private aid dollars to take care of these situations.

As far as how quickly removal of this aid would result in trouble for us, I fully expect that we would see riots in 30 to 60 days if this private funding that we're now relying upon was pulled. There are indications that the people are close to that point. The people know that they are not receiving any aid from the U.S. Government. The people in the camps, the Christians in the camps, they know that they're not receiving any aid from the United States, and they question why is that [sic]. And these are difficult questions for us to answer. Again, we're not sheltered from these. People come directly to our faces every day and ask us about that. So the need for us, it's acute.

STATEMENT OF SHIREEN JERDO IBRAHIM, YAZIDI SURVIVOR OF ISIS ENSLAVEMENT[6]

[The following written statement was provided in addition to Ms. Shireen's testimony.]

Ladies and gentlemen, Members of Congress, thank you for inviting me.

My name is Shireen Jerdo Ibrahim and I am 31 years old. I am one of the thousands of Yazidi survivors. I grew up in Rambusi village, close to Sinjar town, South side of Mount Sinjar. Prior to August 2014, I was living a simple life with my family in our rural area, however, ISIS came and took over our homeland after the withdrawal of Kurdish Peshmerga forces. On August 3rd, 2014, my sister with her children were visiting us and we were preparing to celebrate our mid-summer feast (festival), when I heard the sound of gun-shots from Gerzarek, Seba Sheikh Khider and Tel-Azer (Yazidi complexes, Southern Sinjar), I called my cousin and my uncle, they said that Peshmerga security forces withdrew from the area and that ISIS has attacked our towns. My relatives advised us to escape.

We prepared some stuff and locked the doors of our house. Then we all got into our little pick-up truck and headed toward Sinjar Mountain. By the time we arrived at the foothills of the Mountain, our vehicle broke down, we decided to continue on foot. While we were walking along the road, three cars loaded with ISIS militants arrived and stopped us, they asked all of us to give up weapons and cell phones. I turned off my phone immediately and putted it inside my sock. My family and I among many other Yazidi families were arrested by ISIS and moved to a wedding hall near Sinjar city.

We were ordered and threatened by ISIS militants to get off the trucks they had loaded us into. After we stepped out of the trucks, the militants shot three bullets into a young Yazidi man's head killing him because he said he wanted to wait for his family to arrive. Our

---

6 Practicing an ancient, non-Abrahamic religion, the Yazidis are among the most threatened religious minorities on earth, numbering today approximately 500,000-600,000 people mostly centered in northern Iraq. Accused by ISIS of being "devil worshippers," they were subject to a brutal genocide campaign during the ISIS war beginning in 2014. See: Allison, Christine. "The Yazidis." Oxford Research Encyclopedias, accessed October 2019, https://oxfordre.com/religion/view/10.1093/acrefore/9780199340378.001.0001/acrefore-9780199340378-e-254.

tragedy began from here as they moved all the abducts to the government office inside Sinjar district. ISIS militants separated Yazidi girls for the rest of us by force. My sister, Sahera, was about 15 years old and she was the second girl that was taken. Her hand was in my hand and she was throwing up and crying. She was wearing a dress I had made for her, I was crying and begging them to not take her. One of the militants hit my back with his weapon. Then they forced us all into buses and took us to Badoosh jail.

The jail smelled dirty and there was blood everywhere on the floor. While were all crammed together and terrified, the jail was targeted by US coalition airstrike. As a result, they moved us to Tal-Afar district where ISIS leaders who are responsible for our kidnapping and selling were there. One of them called Haji Mahdi who is from Tel afar and another called Abu Ali from Mosul. I recognized Abu Ali on television when he was escaping from Talafar among IDPs where he was interviewed on Kurdish TV (Rudaw). He is responsible for separating me from my family and selling and enslaving me with many other Yazidi girls. I heard that he now lives in IDPs camp close to Mosul and there is no one to punish him for his crimes against me and against Yazidi community. There are thousands of ISIS militants like Abu Ali who committed crimes against Yazidis and today, they are free without punishment.

From Tel -afar I was sold to a person from Raqa city in Syria, In Raqa they tortured me because I refused to talk. From Raqa they sold me again to a person from Mosul city. I was sold and bought as a cheap commodity for more than five times. Some girls were sold as cheap as few dollars. I spend nine months in captivity under ISIS; it was like hell. They performed an abdominal surgery on me while in Mosul city and until now, I am suffering from the effects of it. I don't know why they operated on me or what kind of a procedure was done on my body. They committed all kinds of atrocious crimes against us including mass killing, sexual enslavement, and forced conversion.

Today as I speak here before you, 19 members of my family and my relatives are missing. They may be killed or still in captivity but we don't know anything about them. Many countries including United states and the United Nations recognized the Yazidi genocide, however our hope was there will be steps following that to provide justice and protection for my people. We are still waiting for action and the liberation of thousands of Yazidis from ISIS captivity. Today, in the liberated areas of Yazidi homeland, there are more than 40 mass graves.

Our homes and lives were destroyed by ISIS, however, we still hope that our homeland will be re-built, so that Yazidis, Christians and other minorities can find peace again, because this was our ancient homeland where we once co-existed as brothers and sisters.

In conclusion, I want to let you know of one thing which I hope you will take serious measures to consider; Yazidis, Christians and other religious minorities, especially the non-Muslim minorities, cannot survive in Syria and Iraq under the current conditions. Without serious action from you and the world governments many of these people will continue to flee their ancient homelands of Syria and Iraq. The protection of these minorities means that one day, my people will not become extinct. Thank you.

As with all tragedies of such a scale as the disappearance of a group of people, there are few parties who are wholly innocent in this story. The roles of political Islam and radical Islamist ideology must be considered in any honest analysis of what has happened to the Christians in the countries under their control. Western foreign policy, international aid policy, and even the actions and behaviors of the Middle Eastern Christians themselves have all played a role in the tragically accelerating decline of the past few decades.[7]

While the story of the Christians in Iraq is the primary focal lens through which the overall disappearance of Christians is examined,

---

[7] Estimates of the Christian population in Iraq as of 2003 were as much as 1.5 million. By 2014, prior to the ISIS war, those estimates were down to approximately 500,000. At present, current estimates are between 125,000 and 200,000. See: U.S. Department of State, Bureau of Democracy, Human Rights and Labor, *Iraq 2018 Religious Freedom Report*. Accessed October 23, 2019. https://www.state.gov/wp-content/uploads/2019/05/IRAQ-2018-INTERNATION-AL-RELIGIOUS-FREEDOM-REPORT.pdf.

other remaining Christian populations of the Middle East, including those waiting for resettlement in the diaspora, will also be woven into the story. While working within the Church over the years, I often traveled to meet with clergy and laypeople from these countries as our stories and work were so often intertwined. Although a comprehensive survey of the endangered nature of Christianity in the Middle East is beyond the scope of this book, the overall pattern, it is hoped, will become clear.

In my own journey, I had first arrived in Iraq in 2007 while the Bush administration reconstruction efforts were underway. As an international transactions lawyer, I signed on to an effort working on various infrastructure efforts within the country, primarily in the Kurdistan Region in the north. In 2010, under a new administration seeking largely to disengage from Iraq, our commercial reasons for being there were nearing an end, and I was dispatched to roll up operations.

As my work was winding down, I made a courtesy call to the recently installed archbishop of Erbil, his Grace Bashar Warda, CSsR (the Redemptorists). I worked closely with many Iraqi Christians during the previous years, and I was reasonably well-known within the community. When I asked the archbishop what I could do to help them on my way out, his reply was characteristic of the blunt charm I would come to know well over the coming years.

"Well," he said, "you Americans have left us quite a mess here. You could stay involved and help me fix it." So began a period of several years of pro bono work where I helped produce feasibility plans, worked to develop commercial interest in the Christian regions, and traveled back and forth between the US and Iraq several times each year.

Then came the ISIS onslaught of 2014, beginning with the storming of Mosul. As reported in *The Guardian* on June 11, 2014, "Iraq is facing its gravest test since the US-led invasion more than a decade ago, after its army capitulated to Islamist insurgents who have seized four cities and pillaged military bases and banks, in a lightning campaign which seems poised to fuel a cross-border insurgency endangering the entire region.... Senior government officials in Baghdad were...shocked, accusing the army of betrayal and claiming the sacking of the city [Mosul] was a strategic disaster that would imperil Iraq's borders.... The developments seriously undermine US claims to have established a unified and competent military after more than a decade of training."[8]

My scheduled trip to Iraq in July was postponed because of the uncertainty surrounding the takeover of Mosul, just over an hour by car from the Kurdish capital of Erbil. Through an uneasy July, where the Kurdish Peshmerga forces held a wary watch in the towns to the east and north of Mosul, the Christians waited. By August, a full-blown crisis had arrived. In another wave of lightning attacks, ISIS fighters blasted their way into the remainder of Nineveh Province so that, by the third week of August, there were nearly one million displaced people fleeing Mosul, Sinjar, and Nineveh, close to 200,000 of them Christians.[9] The pleas for help came almost immediately from all of those that I knew in the Christian community, including the archbishop. But how could I help?

I was fully engaged in multiple projects in the US at the time, and whenever I raised the issue of Iraq with my colleagues and friends, the response was distant, cautious, and, often, afraid. The sheer barbarism and violence of ISIS was being broadcast nonstop. Americans were weary of more horrific news coming from a wounded and failing country.

Still, for reasons that remain unclear to me, and after a period of difficult discernment, I resolved to go. While I tried to rationalize over the futility of it all, I had many of these Iraqis' photos on my wall. They were my friends. They were calling out in dire need. I was sure I could do something, even if I did not know precisely what it was. A long afternoon spent in discussion with an elderly Lithuanian priest at the Franciscan Monastery in Kennebunkport, Maine, helped me to trust in the sense that this call had purpose. He had survived the Nazis and then the Soviets before finally arriving as a refugee in the US many years earlier and understood fully what was at issue both for myself and those I would be trying to serve.

---

[8] See: Martin Chulov, Fazel Hawramy, and Spencer Ackerman, "Iraq army capitulates to Isis militants in four cities," *The Guardian*, June 11, 2014, accessed October 2019, https://www.theguardian.com/world/2014/jun/11/mosul-isis-gunmen-middle-east-states.

[9] See: "Iraq Christians flee as Islamic State takes Qaraqosh," *BBC News*, August 7, 2014, accessed October 23, 2019, https://www.bbc.com/news/world-middle-east-28686998.

By December of 2014, I had cashed in whatever chips I had available, and just after Christmas, I boarded a flight from Boston to Frankfurt then onto Iraq and Erbil. Erbil, at that time, was one of the largest concentrations of displaced people on earth. In a short time, I was fully installed within the staff of the archdiocese, handling every task that any international lawyer might know, and many more that they would not. For better or worse, aside from family and the closest of friends, I left my US world behind for the next four years.

There in northern Iraq, in a country fully at war, I settled in with a handful of clergy, sisters, and laypeople. The responsibility of nearly 150,000 homeless Christians had been laid upon us. We lived oftentimes without power and water, freezing in the winter, scorched and parched in the blazing inferno of summer. Daily, we looked at each other and at the responsibility in front of us. Thousands of desperate and desolate people coming to our door, standing patiently in our simple offices, asking for help. They needed some money for food, help getting medicine, and a place to live or at least to sleep. Through this all, we worked, we persevered, and we prayed. And as each new day would come, we would move through it all over again.

My heart will always be with them, with those who were there in the darkest days and know what happened. This story, in the end, is theirs, and I pray that I will have done them justice in my telling of it.

This book is not intended as an authoritative history. It is instead a story of what happened, and what is happening now, to the Christians of Iraq and the Middle East. It is written, for the most part, from things seen or experienced firsthand. It was not written from the comforts of a research center with regular amenities like power and water, but in the midst of a country at war. Much of it was compiled with written notes or voice memos captured in spare moments when peace and quiet could be found. Such moments were often few and far between.

As the draft manuscript of this book neared completion in the spring and summer of 2019, the streets around the church complex where we lived in Erbil were increasingly patrolled by heavily-armed security teams on the watch for ISIS and other terrorist operators. Warnings of specific threats now followed one after the other. On Easter Sunday, as the world watched, reports were issued out of Sri

Lanka about the bombings of church goers.[10] We all knew that the same evil existed around us, lurking, waiting for an opportunity to kill again. We had all been resigned to its existence and its smoke hung above and around us always.

Perhaps in due time, there will be a more scholarly study of the complex history and environment of the Christians of Iraq. As for us, we were exhausted down to our very marrow after nearly five years of war, displacement, and struggle. In my room in Erbil, I kept a reproduction of Albrecht Dürer's *Saint Jerome in His Study* and wondered if ever there would come a time when any of us could work in such tranquility. But for this book, there was nothing ideal about trying to write it now, except that now is when it is needed. I hope that the reader will understand the stretched circumstances in which we lived and worked and forgive any shortcomings, both in this book and in what we have done, as best they can.

One final word. In January of 2020, just as this book was going to press, a broken and paralyzed Iraq became the open battleground between the U.S. on one side and Iran and its proxies on the other. While the final impact of this conflict may not play out fully for many months or even years, the plight of the Iraqi Christians there will remain, together with their small rays of hope for survival. In whatever state Iraq may exist at the end of the U.S.-Iran showdown, the realities faced by the Christians in this book will need the same understanding and response if they are to avoid a final disappearance in our lifetime.

---

10 See: Sugam Pokharel, Euan McKirdy and Tara John, "Bombs tear through Sri Lankan churches and hotels, killing 250 people," *CNN*, April 25, 2019, accessed October 2019, https://www.cnn.com/2019/04/21/asia/sri-lanka-explosions/index.html.

CHAPTER 1

Among the Displaced

"Something is not right." Fr. Salar, the Chaldean parish priest, spoke to me quietly in English as we both looked at the three women and the young girl. An elderly grandmother, two middle-aged daughters, and the girl, all wrapped up in dusty clothes and scarves. It was January of 2017, and there had been snow in Al-Qosh the night before. They sat, huddled together on the battered couch with a kerosene heater in front of them. The Kurdish security officer, head of the local *Asayish*, stood in the corner of the room, rubbed a hand over his red eyes, and lit a cigarette. South of the town, the Nineveh Plain spread out under a heavy grey sky and across brown and rolling hills that led to Mosul, barely twenty-eight miles in the distance, where the coalition offensive against ISIS raged on.

"She is not speaking the truth," Salar said, nodding towards the one daughter who continued speaking loudly through a frightened smile. "She is afraid."

The women and the girl had been delivered to the *Asayish* office in Al-Qosh late the night before after having been discovered in hiding by the Kurdish *Peshmerga*. They had been in a small remote village northwest of Mosul and were brought to Al-Qosh, where the Kurds thought that Fr. Salar and the Church could take care of them. They were

1

Christians, the women had told the *Peshmerga*, but the Kurds could not understand them clearly. They spoke in a dialect of Sureth[1], a little broken Arabic, and no Kurdish.

Salar and I switched over to speaking a mix of Spanish and Italian, which was our private language when we needed to speak in cover.

"She is afraid to speak in front of this man," said Salar, "but I think she has become Muslim. The others, I believe, are still Christians. But this one has converted, and she is afraid of what it means for her now. But she will not tell us the truth here."

They were yet another group of lost people. As the towns and villages were slowly liberated, as the ISIS fighters retreated and regrouped, these people seemed to show up as if they came from the ground itself. Inevitably, it seemed, they would end up on the doorstep of the church, the place of last refuge. And we would do what we could do.

Two days later, we had this particular family settled into a small apartment in Erbil, and then the truth came out. The old woman had lost her mind during the two years they hid in the remote village of women and children. The rest of the village were Muslim and afraid of ISIS and the war just the same. The men were all gone, taken away, who knew where. The one sister had, at some point, possibly before the war, married a Muslim man and converted. The other sister, still Christian and mother to the young girl, had been a widow for years. The young girl would stay inside and hide whenever ISIS patrols came by. She was now ten and had not been to any kind of school since she was seven. She was beautiful, with a small flower in her hair, but in her eyes, she was stunned.

The mother of the child brought us tea. I sat next to Deacon Shwan, a middle-aged member of the Archdiocese staff who was in discernment for the priesthood, as we explained that they could stay here, that the Church would pay for it and help them with food, and they would be safe as long as they chose to stay.

"The child will need help," said Shwan, looking at me. "She cannot read or write, but also she is very afraid." Her mother looked at us and tried to smile, but the pain on her face pulled her mouth and her eyes

---

[1] Sureth—the neo-Aramaic language spoken by Christians in the north of Iraq.

into a contortion of despair that was emblematic of Iraq. It was everywhere you looked. And while the entire country lay ripped apart and wounded now, for the Christians the horror of ISIS was just one more episode in a never-ending history. War upon war, flight upon flight, terror upon terror. There in the Christian enclave of Ankawa in the north of Erbil, the thousands of displaced families gathered in camps, communal apartments, and half-finished buildings. They waited or fled and increasing numbers of Christians quietly disappeared into the diaspora. We had no way of knowing how many families were still left in the country. How could they be given hope in any kind of future? Was it even honest of us to try?

Down on the street, Shwan looked back up at the walk-up apartment. "We have money, yes?" he asked.

"We will find some more, somewhere," I said.

Shwan looked at me, then back up again, nodded his head and spoke softly. "God will provide. They are safe here now."

The winter wind gusts were hard and cold, blowing us down the street as we headed back to our cars. We had been taking care of tens of thousands of displaced people for over two years with only the scarcest of funds. The cracks and failures were now showing everywhere. Shwan was one of the most centered people I would meet in the entire course of the war. Two years later, he was made priest in the Chaldean Church.[2] Sitting in my car and looking across the street as the rain started, I very much wanted to believe him.

* * *

How does one explain, to another, what it is like to lose everything but one's life and family overnight? To lose one's town, her home, their community, his business, their church, all of their belongings, their future, everything gone from just one day to the next? One August summer night, you are sitting with your family and friends in the back garden patio of the house you have built with your own hands and paid for

---

[2] In 2019, Deacon Shwan would be ordained as a priest in the Chaldean Catholic Church. Although married with several children at the time of his ordination, Shwan was able to be both married and a priest, as is authorized in the Eastern Rite Catholic churches under the *Code of Canons of the Eastern Churches.*

with your own work, looking at the stars, your car in the driveway, your children asleep upstairs, you and your friends drinking tea now, and the low fear lurking underneath everything. Would it come? Really, would it come here?

By the next night, you and your family are fleeing across the desert, and by the following day, you are all sleeping on the burnt grass behind a church with hundreds of others. Two years later, you are living in an 8- by 14-foot box euphemistically known as a "caravan," suitable perhaps as a temporary construction office at a work site, but which you have had to accept as home for your family of six for the last year and a half. There is no water, no toilet, only occasional electricity to provide brief heat in the below-freezing winter, and perhaps, if you had been lucky enough to find an air conditioning unit, some equally brief relief from the 120-degree summer.

It was December of 2016, and I was in Erbil speaking with a German Jesuit Father who was trying to set up online learning programs for the displaced students scattered in the IDP (*Internally Displaced Person*) camps throughout northern Iraq. As with everything in Iraq, very little of it was happening easily or at all. The Jesuit Father talked about the motivation of the potential students and their families. I explained that their futures and their pasts had been blown apart at the same time, and that was how he should look at them, as people who had had their lives blown apart and could not yet see how they would ever come back together.

By that time, the tide was turning against ISIS and the coalition campaign to take back Nineveh was proceeding quickly towards the stronghold of Mosul. Kurdish *Peshmerga* secured Teleskof first and then Batnaya, whose citizens had rushed back to see their town and their homes in the days after the liberation, only to find it mostly flattened, desecrated, and destroyed. They had existed for the past two years on the belief and hope that one day they could return home and begin to live, only to find their homes, their town, and much of their hope, destroyed.

"Father," I said to the priest, "Come to Batnaya. I will take you there, and you will see and understand. I cannot explain it."

Six weeks earlier, I had been with the Chaldean Fathers Aram and Salim as we made our way through the rubble that had been left behind from the final battle for Batnaya just days before. Our assignment that day was to document the historic Chaldean town, in its state, as it was recovered. Beside us was a group of soldiers, Christian members of the Kurdish *Zeravani* units. Concerned that ISIS fighters might still remain underground, and that IEDs and other unexploded ordinance still lay throughout the town, they walked carefully ahead of us, showing the proper paths to take, their weapons at the ready.

The ancient Christian town, whose main church, Mar Kyriakos, dated back to the early 15th century, had been devastated and, in many places, simply pulverized.[3] During their two-year occupation of the town, ISIS fighters had dug their tunnels and cut away walls between buildings—a distinctive tactic ISIS used so they could easily move about from one building to another, making their numbers appear far greater than they actually were. In backyards throughout the town, they had set up networks of crudely-welded rocket launchers. Their crews were guided through instructions issued by lookouts from the modern bell tower next to the original church. Later, when we climbed to the rooftop of the church, one of the few structures left standing, we saw that these ISIS lookouts had fed themselves just days before on US DOD-supplied MREs (meals, ready-to-eat)—just a small part of the supplies taken from the Iraqi army garrison in Mosul when it was abandoned to ISIS in 2014.

All the burrowing and positioning by ISIS resulted in a heavy price for the town when coalition forces began pounding it in late October of 2016. Responding to observation reports that showed the fanatical defenders moving in numbers throughout the town, US air power and artillery, combined with Kurdish *Peshmerga* ground forces, left evidence in Batnaya of nearly every type of weaponry used in the war: aerial bombs, heavy artillery, rocket-propelled grenades and mortars, heavy machine guns, and small arms fire. Walls still standing were pockmarked by bullet holes and shrapnel, blackened by fires and explosions, cracked through from the heave and concussion of the bombs and heavy artillery. Spent shell casings littered the ground.

And yet, the fortress-like structure of Mar Kyriakos seemed to have remained largely intact. ISIS had intended, it was said, to eventually

---

3 See: "Batnaya," *ChaldeanWiki*, accessed October 2019, https://chaldeanwiki.com/Batnaya.

turn it into a mosque. Coalition forces, meanwhile, aware of its historic and cultural importance, had refrained from directly targeting the original main structure and had instead focused firepower on the lookouts in the adjoining bell tower and the attached office buildings.

Fr. Salim had been born in Batnaya, and it was his town. We paused beside a pile of scorched stones and rubble, and he looked down for a moment.

"My home," he said quietly, still looking down. Then he put his head up and looked at me directly with a broken smile. "This was my home. Here." He waved his hands about briefly in a crooked, halting way. I took a picture of him there, and we moved on, through the courtyard, and into the dark coolness of the church.

Instantly we could smell it, the mix of burned wood, spent ammunition, and desecration. The ancient limestone pillars had been covered with spray paint in ISIS graffiti, the stone altars were shot up or knocked to pieces with sledgehammers.[4] The religious paintings and icons had been torn down and burned. The statues of the Virgin Mary and Saint Joseph were posed, bullet riddled, and decapitated. In front of the remains of the altar, a pile of debris had been plowed up as if it were some obscene offering. I took pictures of it all, then we turned away and stepped outside, back into the courtyard.

"Look, Brother Steve," said Fr. Aram, motioning to me. "Come here, look." He took me by the arm and walked me across the courtyard to a small door. "The chapel of the Virgin Mary," he said. "Come, see."

Two of the soldiers stepped ahead and cleared the room first, then motioned us in, looking down and shaking their heads. Inside, the statue of Our Lady stood in the center of the room, decapitated, the outstretched hands hacked off at the wrists, the altar again destroyed

---

4 Limestone is a predominant geological feature of northern Iraq and, when polished, has a marble-like appearance. Its use has been common in buildings and monuments throughout the history of Iraq. See: "The Black Obelisk," The British Museum, Accessed October 2019, https://www.britishmuseum.org/research/collection_online/collection_object_details. aspx?objectId=367012&partId=1.

"Ancient antiquities and Saddam Hussein-era objects returned to Iraq," *U.S. Immigration and Customs Enforcement*, March 26, 2015, Accessed October 2019. https://www.ice.gov/news/releases/ancient-antiquities-and-saddam-hussein-era-objects-returned-iraq.

Photo by Stephen M. Rasche

Fr. Aram Quia, parish priest of Batnaya, listens to a discussion with town elders in the partially restored church of Mar Kyriakos, October, 2019. With the town still under the control of Iranian backed *Hashd* militia, barely thirty families had begun to return. Under more than two years of ISIS control, the church had been left largely intact due to ISIS plans to convert it to a Mosque. Note, however, the bullet holes over the altar archway where ISIS fighters had shot off the Christian cross. Fr. Aram, seeking to visit the US for additional education in counseling to serve his traumatized people, would have his US visa application summarily denied by US consular staff three times without explanation.

and piled up with debris, the ceiling blackened and burned. And on the back wall, more graffiti.

I read it out loud slowly as the strangeness of it settled in.

Ihr scheiss Kreuzslaven wir toten euch alle
Dieses land ist Islamische land. Ihr Schonuzigen das ihr gehort
nicht da hier.

Interior of the Chapel of the Virgin Mary, Batnaya, Nineveh Plain, Northern Iraq, three days after Kurdish Peshmerga forces won back the town from ISIS fighters with heavy US air support. The graffiti on the left side of the wall is in German, written there by German-speaking ISIS fighters.

"What is it?" asked Fr. Aram.

"It's in German," I answered, then translated for him.

"You shit slaves of the cross we will kill you all. This land is Islamic land. Yours truly, you do not belong here."

"And this here," he pointed further up along the wall.

"German also." I read it out loud as well, first in German, then English.

Oh Ihr Kreuzslaven
Ihr habt kein Platz in Islamischenland
Entweder gehst du raus oder wir toten dich.

"Oh, you slaves of the cross. You have no place in the land of Islam. Either get out or we will kill you."

8

Photo by Stephen M. Rasche

Close-up of graffiti written on the wall of the Chapel of Virgin Mary, Batnaya, by German-speaking ISIS fighters. The translation reads "Oh you slaves of the cross, You have no place in the Land of Islam. Either get out of here or we will kill you."

I stood there looking at the wall, trying to work through the possibilities. Who were these people, really? What had this war become? I stood for a while then shook my head and took pictures of it all, telling Fr. Aram that this would be evidence and he must make sure it was not painted over.

We walked back through the courtyard and outside again, our shoes crunching on the glass and cinders beneath us. Just a kilometer to the south, at the new coalition frontline north of Telkayf, a 155-howitzer thumped once, its rolling shock rumbling across the plain. Then utter stillness all around. That was Batnaya in November of 2016. Not even sparrows lived there anymore.

* * *

IN DECEMBER OF 2016, the German priest arrived at the church rectory at the Chaldean Catholic Diocese of Al-Qosh, whose territory included the town of Batnaya. I had a room there at the time, together with the priests and bishop of the diocese. In their 2014 advance from Mosul, just twenty-eight miles to the south, ISIS had been halted outside Al-Qosh. Throughout the war, Al-Qosh had remained a haven for the displaced Christians who had fled for their lives, pressed up against the mountains, looking down over the vast expanse of the Nineveh Plain. High above the town, built into the sides of a steep rock canyon in 640 CE, perched the monastery of Mar Hormizd. Down below, on the slopes just north of the town center, a twenty-foot lighted cross had continued shining throughout the war, visible for miles from the plains to the south. When some worried that it might provide a target, or provoke ISIS attacks, the Church and the town elders refused to take it down. "We are here," Fr. Aram had said when I first asked about it. "We should let them know, we are here, and we are still here."

Fr. Aram and I greeted the German on the steps and took him in for tea with Bishop Mikha, who was a gracious and kindly old man, always welcoming to visitors. We chatted briefly, finished our tea, and climbed into the Toyota Hi-Lux, the vehicle shared by the priests. I put the German in the front seat, and off we drove, south towards Batnaya and the reality of the war.

I did not speak much during the remainder of the trip, allowing the two priests to speak to one another directly as brother priests, letting Fr. Aram explain the recent history of things in his own way. He had been there throughout the conflict and had stayed in Al-Qosh in August of 2014 with the group of local men who were prepared to defend it to the death if necessary. Still a young priest in his thirties, native to Al-Qosh, he had provided regular assistance to the coalition efforts and knew every stretch of land, every trench, every date on which something had happened.

As we sped south under the heavy grey winter sky, the biblical plains stretching out in every direction, all of the grass brown and matted, the road began to rise gently as we came upon Batnaya. The first collapsed buildings, the roadsides heaped with plowed over trucks and cars, mangled and burned, all of it slowly came into view. No work had been done since our first visit, the only difference being that the town had been declared cleared of ISIS fighters and soldiers, so escorts were no longer needed. But no one had returned aside from brief visits to see what was left of their homes. Essentially, we were alone in a destroyed town that once held 6,000 people.

Fr. Aram led the German around the town, to the church, and then to the Chapel of the Virgin Mary, where nothing had been touched and the graffiti still remained as we had first found it. When they came out, the German stopped, shaking his head slowly.

"I have no words," he pled, his sad eyes looking at me. "I am grateful you have brought me here. I am changed by this, but I have no words."

I have a picture of the two priests taken just then, standing amidst the rubble and debris of the church courtyard, the tall German looking older and deeply sad behind a weak smile, and Fr. Aram standing somberly in his full cassock against the winter chill, a young face grown old from having seen so much, a face for which very little else in this life would come as a surprise.

In 2015, Fr. Aram opened a trauma center in Al-Qosh using private funds and small donations, seeking to restore some peace to the destroyed lives of the people. In furtherance of this, he had attempted to further his formal education in the US to improve upon his professional counseling skills and then return to Iraq and serve his people. His bishop and the Chaldean Church in the US formally assured immigration officials of the Church's intent to accept full responsibility for his stay and guaranteed his return to Iraq. Unimpressed in the years to follow, the visa section at the US consulate in Erbil would summarily deny his application three times.

* * *

"THE AREA HAS NOT BEEN CLEARED," the Iraqi colonel told me, waving toward the church compound of Mar Addai there in the center of Karemlesh. A freshly-painted Humvee with Iraqi markings roared by, its suspension modified to lower its profile. "It's not safe to go in."

He had been educated in Texas and spoke perfect English. Fr. Thabet, the parish priest of the town, answered him in Arabic while the seminarian, Deacon Wael, stood next to them. A small group of Iraqi soldiers in desert camouflage stood to the side, their weapons slung over their shoulders. Behind them stood Christian members of the Nineveh Protection Unit (NPU), a small Christian militia which had been formed in support of the recovery of Nineveh.

The Christian town of Karemlesh had been liberated from ISIS occupiers by the Iraqi army after a fierce battle just days before, on October 26, 2016. It was a town whose rich history traced well back into the time of the ancient Assyrians. In 1846, it had been the site of early excavations by the then thirty-year-old English archaeologist and later diplomat and politician, Austen Henry Layard. In 331 BCE, Alexander the Great had fought and won a great battle over the Persian Emperor Darius III on the plains surrounding this town. And in 1743 CE, the Persians under Nader Shah had bombarded and overrun the town, which was by then an important trade center, during the Mesopotamian campaign of the Persians against the Ottomans, leaving behind thousands of massacred Assyrian Christians in their wake.

In the late October 2016 battle against ISIS, there were no Christians left in the town to harm. The entire population had fled over two years earlier as ISIS rampaged up the road from Mosul, just eighteen miles to the northwest. But the fight, which involved elements of the Iraqi army along with substantial US air support, had left much of the town burned and destroyed. Fr. Thabet had been there on October 26, the same day of the liberation, to raise a temporary cross on the hill of the St. Barbara monastery and shrine just across the main road from the town. But on that day, he had been denied access to the town and the church, with the Iraqi forces still concerned about booby traps, IEDs, and remnant ISIS fighters crawling up from their tunnel mazes.

Now, three days later, it appeared we would still not be let into the church compound. The Iraqi colonel, who was part of the army medical corps, explained that the main forces had already moved ahead. It was unclear who would be coming in next to handle the official security and demining of the town now that ISIS had been pushed out. After twenty minutes of dialogue back and forth, now including the head of the NPU group, it was agreed that we could enter the church compound and view the immediate surrounding area through a limited street route with an armed member of the NPU, but if anything happened, it would be on us.

For Fr. Thabet and the Church, getting into the parish compound and viewing the neighborhoods as early as possible was critical—not just for the purpose of giving positive news and support to the anxious residents waiting in exile back in Erbil, but also for the purpose of documenting its condition, ahead of any further activity in the town. Left unsaid, but clearly in the background of the earlier conversation, was the concern that property would be looted under the guise of protection before Fr. Thabet and his people would have a chance to get in.

A middle-aged volunteer from the NPU, dressed in loose-fitting green camouflage, no helmet or body armor, and with an ancient Kalashnikov[5] leveled in front of him, led the way. We followed him carefully through the front gate of the courtyard. Inside was a heap of tires that was meant to be set aflame by ISIS to provide a smoke screen during street fighting. Slowly, we walked to the side door of the sanctuary of Mar Addai. The door, hanging askew, had already been forced open, but it was impossible to tell when. We stepped inside after the NPU guard and stood for a moment, allowing our eyes to adjust. The sunlight slanted in through the blown-out windows, and slowly we started to see it all.

The marauders had tried to burn out the church above the altar and off to the far side of the sanctuary. We could smell it before we could see it clearly. The cupola and the apse were blackened, as was most of the ceiling throughout the main sanctuary.[6] The main stone altar had been knocked down and broken into pieces. The stone edifices, which displayed Christian markings, were pockmarked with bullet scars. Just behind the remains of the altar, facing the main sanctuary, the statue of the Virgin Mary stood—clearly positioned there intentionally, decapitated, and hands cut off at the wrists. Below, off to the side of the crossing, the remains of the statue of Saint Joseph stood in a shattered stump, riddled with bullet holes. The head and upper torso were completely shot off.

Fr. Thabet moved slowly to the altar of his church and looked down at the ruin, then up and out to the rest of the sanctuary, his eyes struggling. The four of us looked around, but no one spoke. The priest and the deacon walked over to the side passage and into a small shrine where the remains of earlier priests had been buried. Inside was the martyr, Fr. Ragheed Ganni, who had been murdered by Islamic terrorists just

---

5 The Kalashnikov rifle, often referred to as the AK-47, is originally a Soviet-designed weapon and now widely distributed throughout the world. See: David Blair, "AK-47 Kalashnikov: The firearm which has killed more people than any other," *The Telegraph*, July 2, 2015, accessed October 2019, https://www.telegraph.co.uk/news/worldnews/northamerica/usa/11714558/AK-47-Kalashnikov-The-firearm-which-has-killed-more-people-than-any-other.html.

6 The cupola is a small dome-like structure commonly found in Eastern Christian churches over the altar. The apse refers to the semi-circular area behind the altar.

outside the Holy Spirit church in Mosul, along with three of his deacons in June of 2007.

Eyewitness accounts from Fr. Ragheed's parish told the story of his last hours. It was Sunday, June 3, 2007, and the Church had already made plans to move him out of Mosul, as a result of the continuing threats against him by Islamic terror groups. They wanted to force him to stop saying Mass. Fellow priests had pleaded with Fr. Ragheed for months to leave Mosul, but the priest had refused, always insisting that he could not deny the church to the faithful who were still there. Eventually, his brothers in the Church were able to persuade him to depart, at least temporarily, for a safer parish in the diaspora outside Iraq. The next day, Monday June 4th, he had been scheduled to move to Erbil and begin the process of applying for foreign visas. But on that Sunday, there were still members of his congregation to be served.

The situation in Mosul had grown full of danger due to the conflicts between the attempts from the Maliki-led government in the south to impose Shia control over a historically Sunni-majority city. The historic animosity between the two factions led to deadly expression from the Sunnis in the Al-Qaeda splinter groups, who were operating with increasing freedom and aggression, throughout the city. And in this vortex of hate and violence, the Christians were an easy target for expressing the power of Islamic terror.

On that day, many of the roads through the city were already closed, and traffic was diverted through numerous checkpoints. When the faithful arrived, Fr. Ragheed began the Mass and gave communion, but the service was hurried due to the danger that surrounded the church. When the Mass ended, Fr. Ragheed stepped into a waiting car with one of his deacons, and they began to pull away from the church, followed by a second car carrying two more of the deacons and one of their wives.

The two cars had just barely pulled out when suddenly another car stormed in front of the departing cars, screeching to a halt and blocking their way. Four masked gunmen jumped out, dressed in black, armed with Kalashnikovs. In pairs, the gunmen approached each of the two cars and pointed their weapons at the passengers inside. Recognizing Fr. Ragheed, they yelled at him to get out of the car.

Fr. Ragheed asked them who they were and what they wanted. Witnesses recall the gunmen yelling that they were with *Ansar al-Sunna*, one of the many Sunni Muslim insurgent groups that had been fighting against the US throughout Iraq while simultaneously seeking to impose their own vision of Islam on the areas under their control. *Jamaat Ansar al-Sunna* (Assembly of the Helpers of Sunna) was behind the 2004 suicide bombing attacks against government buildings in Erbil that killed over one hundred people. In Mosul, they had engaged in fierce fighting with the US Army in 2004, including multiple suicide bombing attacks. Beyond suicide attacks, they were equally notorious for the kidnappings and beheadings displayed on the internet worldwide.[7]

Pointing directly at Fr. Ragheed, they continued yelling at him to get out of the car, shouting, "How many times did we tell you to close this church? How many times did we tell you not to pray in this church?"

"How can we close a house of prayer that helps the poor?" answered the priest.

The gunmen then dragged Fr. Ragheed and the deacon across the street and told them to say their final prayers. As the two stood there, the gunmen shouted out *Allahu Akhbar* and then emptied their magazines. One of the remaining deacons then rushed forward to the bullet-riddled bodies but was cut down immediately. The gunmen turned their fire on the remaining deacon. All three deacons, Waheed Hanna Isho'a, Bassman Yousef Daoud, and Gassan Issam Bidawid, died on the street with Fr. Ragheed. A funeral for the four men was held the next day at the church of Mar Addai in Karemlesh, with thousands attending from the Christian community throughout the Nineveh Plain and Erbil.[8]

In November 2016, when our group first saw the squared-off hole in the floor of Mar Addai, we thought it must be the entrance to another ISIS tunnel. Standing at its edge, Fr. Thabet looked at the floor beside him and suddenly realized what it was. A body had been exhumed there. The remains of the wooden casket lay in pieces on the floor underneath

---

[7] See: "Ansar al-Sunna (AS)," *The Investigative Project on Terrorism*, accessed October 2019, https://www.investigativeproject.org/profile/125/ansar-al-sunna-as.

[8] In May, 2018, the Vatican's Congregation for the Causes of Saints formally opened the canonization cause of Fr. Ganni and the three murdered deacons. The author serves as official member of the Historical Commission for the Vatican Postulator in the ongoing cause.

Photo by Stephen M. Rasche

Fr. Thabet Habib on his first return to his church, Mar Addai, in the town of Karem-lesh, Nineveh Plain, Northern Iraq, November, 2016. The town had been won back from ISIS control by Iraqi forces with US air support just days earlier, and remnant ISIS fighters were believed to be still in tunnels on the outskirts of the town.

the dusty shreds of the burial vestments. But of the human remains, there were none to be found, no bones anywhere.

"They have taken him," said Fr. Thabet. "But they have taken the wrong Fr. Ganni."

He stood up straight and pointed several feet away.

"Fr. Ganni, the martyr, he is here." He was pointing to a marker barely visible beneath a pile of debris.

"This Fr. Ganni, they have taken. He was the cousin of Fr. Ganni, the martyr. But this one was killed in a car crash at another time."

"What will they do with his bones?" I asked.

"These people," said Thabet, "they are crazy. Who can understand this, what they do?"

I took pictures of it all, and we walked into the burned-out sacristy, where Fr. Thabet and Deacon Wael poked in the ashes, looking for the remains of any liturgical items that could still be salvaged. We gathered as much as we could find into a small pile, which we placed on a pew out in the sanctuary. We then gathered up our collection of burned, twisted metal and tattered liturgical texts and brought them back outside to Thabet's car.

He looked over back into the courtyard and to the rectory. He then spoke to the NPU guard, who shook his head and answered back in Sureth.

"The Iraqi army has cleared the building, but he has not been inside," said Thabet. "He says that we must be careful where we step."

Inside, the rooms had been ransacked, the shelves pulled down, the drawers dumped out, and the beds turned over. The exterior windows and doors had all been blown out from the concussion of the aerial bomb that had left a twenty-yard crater across the street. But there had been no fire inside, no shooting, it seemed. Then the NPU guard stopped and pointed to what appeared to be a small cylinder made of fabric and filled with lead shot, used as a hand weight for exercising. It had been placed just inside a doorstep. The guard spoke to Fr. Thabet, who looked up to me.

"He is saying it is a bomb. Of plastic explosives. When you step on it, it will explode. He says they have found many of them in the town." We moved warily past it, finding three more before we made our way back out the front door. We climbed into Thabet's car and drove slowly through the neighborhood surrounding the church. He pulled the car over after a few minutes and walked alone out to the flattened remains of his family home. He stared down for several minutes, then we all got back in the car and drove away. The sun was slanting low as we made our way back east, past the checkpoints, past the bombed-out ghost towns, and back to Erbil.

17

CHAPTER 2

Hoping for Change

I t was November 9, 2016, and there would be three of us in the car that day. Me and the two Chaldean priests, Fr. Thabet of Karamlesh, and Fr. Salim. Fr. Salim was the senior priest on the pastoral staff at the Archdiocese of Erbil, where he served as the parish priest at Mar Gorgis. Mar Gorgis is the oldest church in Ankawa, with existing evidence indicating its original structure may trace back as far as the 9th century CE.[1]

We met at Mar Gorgis at dawn on a chilly morning for a simple breakfast of tea and bread and then headed west to Nineveh to continue our documentation of the recovered Christian towns. Fr. Thabet had recovered in spirits after our sobering trip two days earlier to his church in Karemlesh. Today, with Fr. Salim at the wheel of his Kia SUV, there was only one topic of discussion for the entire three-hour drive across the northern edge of the Nineveh Plain—the US presidential election.

We were eight hours ahead of US Eastern Standard Time, and the election returns were still coming in. While the election results were still very much uncertain in the US, one thing was abundantly clear among the Christians of Iraq: they were in support of Donald Trump. Shocking as it continues to be for supporters of President Obama, his

---

[1] See: "Mar Gewargis Church in Ankawa," *Mesopotamia Heritage*, accessed October 2019, https://www.mesopotamiaheritage.org/en/monuments/leglise-mar-guorguis-dankawa/.

presidency was viewed as a disaster by the Iraqi Christians. The line often spoken was that "Bush has blood on his hands for the way he came in, but Obama has blood on his hands for the way he went out."

From the perspective of the Iraqi Christians, the American invasion of 2003 under George W. Bush set in motion the tearing apart of a country in which the Christians, without any power faction to protect them, were left as easy prey to fanatics and gangsters. During the years of American military administration in Iraq, Christian churches were regularly bombed and terrorized, leaders were kidnapped and murdered. Thousands of Christians abandoned Baghdad and the south of Iraq and moved north to the long-standing Christian enclaves of Erbil and Nineveh. And yet, as bad as that situation was, the Christians still held on to hope that there was a commitment from the US to Iraq that would be not only political but moral as well. According to Bob Woodward's *Plan of Attack*, US Secretary of State Colin Powell had warned President Bush prior to the Iraq invasion, "You are going to be the proud owner of 25 million people. You will own all their hopes, aspirations, and problems. You'll own it all."[2] For the Iraqi Christians, this truth remained, and they held on to every expectation that the Americans would stay in place to fix what they had broken, which included the safety of the Christians.

Whatever expectation the Iraqi Christians had of long-term support from the US soon evaporated with the new policy direction of the Obama administration in 2008. During his run-up to the November election, Obama called the Bush action in Iraq a "dumb war, a rash war," and vowed, as a campaign promise, to end it "responsibly."[3] The Christians agreed with Obama; the opening of the war had been both dumb and rash at best, and far worse in many other aspects. But as for ending the war "responsibly," the Christians saw that as meaning something completely different than the political expediency of Obama's full withdrawal that took place between 2010 and 2011.

"Your country," an Iraqi Christian politician wagged his finger at me in January of 2015, "came into our country, destroyed it, and then left us,

---

2 Woodward,B. (2004). *Plan of Attack*. New York, NY: Simon and Schuster, p. 150.

3 Greg Jaffe, "Obama's Legacy, 'Tell me how this ends': Obama's struggle with the hard questions of war," *Washington Post*, June 3, 2016, accessed October, 2019, https://www.washingtonpost.com/graphics/national/obama-legacy-ending-war-in-iraq.html.

even the innocent and the helpless, to heal ourselves. Have you read the speech from your president with Maliki when you Americans left? It is," he waved his hands and fluttered his fingers, "fairy tales."

In retrospect, the remarks of President Obama welcoming Iraqi Prime Minister Al-Maliki to the White House on December 12, 2011, appear at best as naïve platitudes, referring loftily to the new existence of a "sovereign, self-reliant, and democratic Iraq." As the next three years would so disastrously prove, Iraq, especially under Al-Maliki, was none of these things. In fact, Iraq was an increasingly fractured state, rife with corruption inside a barely functioning government, with a military and security structure that was merely a shell serving to siphon funds for private wealth. Even worse, under Al-Maliki, the ruling government openly sought to marginalize the Sunni people, thereby laying the foundation for initial support of ISIS by the disaffected Sunni populations, most of those from the north and in Mosul.

For the Christians, foreseeing the violence that lay ahead was not any act of great clairvoyance, and the ignoring of this reality by the US was not based in lack of knowledge or intelligence to the contrary. In the view of the Christians, the truth was that the US decision to pull out was a mere political calculation from an administration that did not care about the imperiled lives it was leaving behind. As the Iraqi politician had put it to me, "Your campaign promises, our lives."

Later, in the aftermath of the ISIS attacks, the displaced Christians of Iraq expected that there would finally be some acknowledgment and support for their plight from the US government. Instead, they found themselves continually rebuffed by rote answers from US officials—the US was contributing heavily in humanitarian aid to Iraq, all US aid was implemented through the UN and USAID, and this aid was being effectively distributed in line with well-established policy guidelines.

In practice, for the Christians, this meant they received nothing due to the "needs-based" standards adhered to by the UN and USAID and under which the displaced Christians were determined to be at a lesser "need" than other displaced persons in the region. At a threshold level, and from a process perspective, the pushback from these two appeared straightforward. For both the UN and USAID, and nearly all other Western and EU aid agencies, humanitarian assistance was fundamentally grounded in this "needs-based" analysis. This focus, laudable in many respects, was designed to ensure that aid reached those most in need, regardless of age, gender, race, disability, and a range of other potential factors. In short, this approach asserted that aid is most fairly applied when it is focused on the actual needs of the individual, as opposed to his or her community or group. In theory, much of this made sense. In the established policy paradigm of the UN and USAID, it had become a bedrock principle that was beyond questioning. As a senior USAID official in Washington, DC, told me and a congressional aide in an informational meeting in September of 2016, "We will never move away from needs-based. It will never happen."

The problem for the Christians was that the implementation of the early help they received from private, faith-based donors around the world had, in an ironic sense, simply been too efficient. Working with the flexibility to adapt to the reality of the situation and having almost zero overhead costs due to the existing mission-oriented structure of their staff, the Church-managed efforts had led to a situation where, by most objective measures, on an individual needs basis, the displaced Christians were in better condition than the displaced Muslim and Yazidi populations. Notably, these populations were solely reliant on the far slower and much less efficient UN and USAID driven programs, which routinely saw overhead costs reach 40 percent or more.

But by one measure, and in many ways the most crucial one, Christians remained one of the two most vulnerable groups in Iraq. In population numbers, as a distinct minority group, they were already on the verge of disappearing, the brutally abused and beaten Yazidi population not far behind. With a population approaching 1.5 million at the outset of the US invasion in 2003, the Christians, in 2016, were now down to an estimate of no more than 350,000, and dozens of families were leaving the country every day.[4] The genocide designation in March of 2016, wrenched out from the Obama State Department at the last

---

[4] Beginning with the onset of the ISIS attacks in the summer of 2014, accurate population numbers for displaced populations were difficult to obtain. No serious government or other census efforts were made during this time. The Christians in particular were an extremely fluid and transient population, with many leaving the country every month, or moving between towns. Throughout, the church sought to maintain general numbers through informal surveys within the church communities in Iraq. The figures noted here reflect that effort.

minute under a barrage of public pressure, had so far seen no change in treatment for either the Christians or the Yazidis. If anything, the departure of Christians from the country was accelerating.

Looking every day to help bridge this gap, we continued to seek support from the UN mission in Erbil. Andrew Walther, vice president of communications for the Knights of Columbus, who was visiting with us in Erbil in late May of 2016, accompanied me to a meeting with the newly-arrived head of UNOCHA (UN Office for Coordination of Human Affairs) for the Kurdistan Region of Iraq, hoping to make some progress for our cause.

"The problem," she said with apparent and honest sympathy, "is that you have done too good a job with your people."

When countered with the argument that the Iraqi Christians, as a people, were on the verge of extinction and that the private funds keeping them in the country could not be sustained, her response seemed genuine.

"Our problem is that we do not have enough money even to take care of the people we have now. We are short on funding goals for everything on our budget. If you run out of funds and your people present themselves at our camps, we will take them in."

"They will never go into the UN camps, they are afraid they will be attacked there," I answered. "They will never trust the Muslims, not in this situation. If that becomes the only option, they will all just leave. That is what we are facing. We are trying to keep a population together. That is what we need help with. We can continue seeking private donations, but we need some bigger help to hold things together."

She was sorry, and I believed her. "Well," said Andrew, when we stepped outside, "that answers that. Now at least we know." When we returned to the rectory at the archdiocese and explained to the archbishop how the meeting had gone, he simply frowned and then looked out the window.

"Nothing," he said quietly. "Always nothing."

The archbishop, it was clear, had already given up hope of receiving any help from the Americans or the UN. Looking back, there were many steps along the way that eroded the hopes Christian leaders held for help from the Obama administration. But they crystallized in a

March 2016 closed-door meeting with Assistant Secretary of State Tom Malinowski. Accompanied by an entourage of State Department staffers from Washington, DC, and members of the US embassy and consulate in Iraq, Malinowski sat in the conference room of the Archdiocese of Erbil, facing squarely the four primary bishops of the Christian churches in northern Iraq. At the end of the table, I sat beside Archbishop Warda, quietly taking notes.

The purpose of the visit, said Malinowski, was to advise the bishops that the hoped-for genocide declaration was unlikely to come, and that it would be best for everyone to focus on what could be done rather than on things that were not possible. He explained that, soon, the offensive against ISIS would begin, and that the towns of Nineveh were expected to be eventually recovered. He wanted to assure the bishops that the US would help them in every way possible, and in furtherance of that, he wanted to hear from them.

With that, each bishop spoke in turn, all with a variation of the same theme.

"Thank you for coming. We appreciate your kind words, but in two years, we have received, so far from you Americans, nothing but words. We are losing more of our people every day, and you are doing nothing to help us with this. We will disappear soon. When will you help us?"

Malinowski, polished, professional, and gentle, stated he was grateful to hear all of their concerns and that the US would do everything possible to help them return when the time came. Then, without shifting a note in his delivery, he looked at the four bishops and said, "One important priority for the US is that, in the recovery of territory, there are not reprisals against the Sunni Muslim population."

At first, I thought I must have misheard, but Malinowski continued, speaking about how the Sunnis had been victims of the war and ISIS as well. As he went on, it seemed clear that this was not simply one offering of information among many; it was instead a structured position that was now being delivered to an audience that had no idea why they were being asked to listen.

Archbishop Warda sat to the end without comment, then translated for his fellow bishops, who stared ahead blankly, impassive.

"I think," said Nicodemus Daoud Sharaf, the Orthodox archbishop of Mosul, in a confused, almost stunned voice, "you are speaking to the wrong people."

"The Sunnis," Archbishop Warda said evenly, "have nothing to fear from the Christians, I assure you. We are not the perpetrators of any of this violence."

With that, the meeting wound up rather quickly, and off they went in a phalanx of bearded, rough-looking Americans.

Standing on the doorstep of the rectory, I looked over at Archbishop Warda.

"I thought you would get angry with him."

"Ah," he said shaking his head quickly. "We expect this by now from these people. They will not help us."

Days later, in contrast to every indication given by Malinowski, Secretary of State John Kerry announced a finding of genocide against the Christians, Yazidis, and other victims of ISIS. The arguments, by various groups, against including the Christians in this declaration, arguments which continued right up to the final days before the announcement, were, in the end, battered into submission by the undeniable truths documented in an almost 300-page brief funded and coordinated by the Knights of Columbus. Earlier, they had sent one of their staff attorneys to stay with us and conduct interviews throughout the displaced person camps in Erbil.

The genocide declaration served as an initial shot in the arm to the Christian community of Iraq and its supporters around the world. But in the months to follow, the realization began to grow that whatever moral worth the declaration may have had, it did not mean that anything was really going to change. The policy line at USAID and the UN remained the same—they were governed by a needs-based assessment for individuals. The genocide declaration, they maintained, had changed nothing, and from the Obama administration came nothing to address the dwindling population of Christians in Iraq.

Cumulatively, the Christian people knew their help was not coming from the US or the UN, only from private groups, nearly all of which were affiliated with the church in some way. As the US elections drew closer, Iraqi Christians saw Hillary Clinton as a continuation of the abandonment they felt under the Obama administration. Furthermore, the view was widespread that any Clinton administration policy would be under the heavy influence of Saudi Arabia and the Gulf Arab states, as a result of the tens of millions of dollars they had donated to the Clinton Foundation in the run-up years to the election.[5]

The Trump campaign, on the other hand, had been regularly speaking about the plight of Mideast Christians throughout the summer and into the fall of 2016, together with regular denunciations of, what his campaign labeled openly as "radical Islamic terror." These pledges were translated and spread daily throughout the Christian community in Iraq, and whatever liabilities and faults candidate Trump may have been dragging around with him as an individual, his words struck home for the Christians who felt they never had anyone to speak out on their behalf under President Obama. By Election Day in the US, the Iraqi Christians were in total support of Donald Trump.

As we drove along that morning, around the cutouts in the blown-up roads, through checkpoint after checkpoint, past scarred and abandoned villages, and out into the open plain, I pulled in wireless signals sporadically. I'd receive text messages from friends in the US who updated me on the progress of the election. By 11 a.m. in Iraq on November 9, 2016, Donald Trump had been declared the winner, and Christians all across the country reacted with jubilation. Legitimate hope, they believed at the time, had finally returned.

---

5 Jeff Stein, "4 experts make the case that the Clinton Foundation's fundraising was troubling," *Vox*, August 25, 2016, accessed October, 2019, https://www.vox.com/2016/8/25/12615340/hillary-clinton-foundation.

CHAPTER 3

I Should Have Listened

Thamir and his wife had both been born in Batnaya. When ISIS stormed up the road and into their town in August of 2014, they fled north with their three young daughters to Al-Qosh. There, they remained, displaced and dependent on the charity of the church and friends, for the next two years. Throughout this time, Thamir was in regular contact with the rest of his family members, all of them now in Australia. Every call was the same—his relatives pleading with him to emigrate any way possible and join them there, and Thamir insisting that Batnaya was his home and he would not abandon it. He would wait and be one of the first to return, they would see.

In November of 2016, when ISIS was finally driven out of Batnaya, Thamir was there, one of the first to re-enter the town. To his relief, he found that his home was one of the few still standing, even if all the windows and doors had been blown out and the interior, gutted and looted. When he viewed the rest of his town, all around him was devastation and ruin. Their church, the noble ancient structure of Mar Kyriakos, had survived. Thamir looked around at the group of men who also came to view their homes, and there, in the courtyard of the church, under the guidance of the priests who held them together during displacement, they formed their plans and began to work.

The first obstacle was lack of power and water. The focus of the coalition forces was now Telkayf and Mosul. The restoration and rehabilitation of the recovered towns would be for another group at some future time. Pleas for infrastructure help to the Iraqi and Kurdish government were met with Kafkaesque responses: There are no people who have returned to Batnaya, the governments responded, and they cannot use resources on towns that are empty. We responded that the towns were empty because we have no power or water to rebuild our homes.

Exchanges of this sort were now becoming a pattern we would see repeatedly over the course of 2016 and into early 2017. Whenever approached by the Church for help in resolving these recurrent impasses, both the UN and USAID officials in Iraq and Washington, DC, responded similarly—they are working through the local officials and addressing priorities according to their assessments. This was standard policy, the UN and USAID officials advised. When countered with the reality that this was still a war zone, and that there were no real local authorities withstanding in the community other than the Church, the Western officials dug in, restated the established process, and said they were in full cooperation with the government in Baghdad.

I had been dispatched by the Church in the midst of this to bring our case directly to US and UN officials in Washington, DC, and New York. And so, in the fall of 2016, began a period of shuttling between Iraq and the US. There it was explained to me that the policy of the Obama administration had been to make the branding of the restoration and recovery as outwardly belonging to the Iraqi government. As such, even if the local government authority was not clear, it was necessary to give it support as if it were. As the days wore on, and I moved from one well-appointed, heavily secured government office to another, two motives and their accompanying narratives began to emerge.

Officially, the effort was designed to rebuild the confidence of the Iraqi people in their government—a confidence which had been shattered in the summer of 2014 by the humiliating and panic-stricken retreat of the Iraqi army in the face of vastly smaller numbers of raging ISIS fanatics. In essence, by quietly allowing US and UN aid funding to prominently display the flag of the Iraqi government, it was hoped that the people of Iraq would begin to sense some competence and coherence in the fragile Iraqi central government, thus helping to speed up the recovery process and move it more rapidly away from the continuing cloud of chaos and incompetence which remained over Baghdad. The political appointees from the Obama administration invariably stuck to this line.

But occasionally, a long-term career official that had survived through the changeovers of administrations before would take me aside and tell a different story.

"Mostly, it's a smoke screen," the USAID career manager told me as we sat in a coffee shop a few blocks from his office in the Ronald Reagan Building.

"Of course, like all good smoke screens, there's a little bit of fire to it," he continued. "Yes, this [Obama] administration does believe that the US brand is not one that always helps, and yes, the plan to give credit to the Iraqi government does, in theory, have some merit. But that's not all of what is really behind this. What's really behind it is, if this administration showed that these were *really* US-funded efforts, and if we took control of them, even if to make sure they were *really* working, the optics of it would be a disaster for the president. Remember, the president took us out of Iraq, rightly or wrongly, and he owns that. Now here we are just a few years later, having to rebuild towns that were destroyed by a bunch of gangsters using weapons we left behind for the Iraqi army. Understand here, the less our fingerprints are on any of this the better." In the slow, almost halting transition of new management personnel into the Trump administration, the holdover staff from the Obama years kept to their positions.

Meanwhile in Batnaya, the Church continued to receive funding and support from private organizations and sympathizers around the world. Fr. Salar Kajo, a native of Al-Qosh, back now from eight years in Rome where he had received a doctorate in canon law, was given the responsibility of managing the Church-funded rebuilding process by his bishop, and the Chaldean patriarch in Baghdad. He quickly assembled a team from the people of Batnaya. They began to work using makeshift generators and water tanker trucks hired either with their meager funds or, oftentimes, donated. There, from the beginning, was Thamir, ever a smile on his face, filled with the positive work of taking back his home and his town. Their goal was to reopen the church for Holy Week and Easter services in the spring of 2017.

All through those months, the people worked, clearing the debris from the streets, cleaning their church. Those who could be were there every day, including Thamir. Families who had been living in Erbil or Dohuk came on weekends and began recovering their homes, if they were still standing. If not, then they would help their neighbors or the Church. Very quickly, one danger became apparent: the town was filled with unexploded ordnance, commonly known as UXOs. Children were picking them up in their backyards and bringing them to their parents, who were then placing them on the sidewalks outside their homes where they hoped, somehow, somebody in charge of such things would have them removed.

Fr. Salar and the elders went to the Kurdish forces outside the town to ask for help but were told by the Kurds that it was not their priority. The enemy was still out in front, and that was where they were headed. Demining was the problem of the federal government, or somebody else, in any case. The Iraqi army forces, meanwhile, were engaged in constant and heavy fighting to the south and west of Mosul. Batnaya, they said, was a Kurdish problem, or somebody else's. But the people of Batnaya were turning up more UXOs every day, and it was just a matter of time before something tragic would happen.

I knew from my prior discussions with the UN that they had a significant budget for demining at the United Nations Mine Action Service (UNMAS). At minimum, they had educational materials that we could post in the town and instructional pamphlets in Arabic that we could give out to the people. After a few phone calls, a meeting was set up, so I headed off across the northern edge of Nineveh, east to the United Nations Assistance Mission Iraq (UNAMI) compound in Erbil.

There were three others there when I arrived inside the UNMAS office: the local staff manager, his assistant, and a member of the international staff. After introductions and an explanation of the situation, the local manager began speaking in fluent but heavily-accented English.

"The problem we have is one of jurisdiction," he said.

"Technically, Batnaya is not part of the Kurdistan Region but belongs instead under the jurisdiction of the Iraqi forces. Presently, however, the Kurdish forces are there. Logistically, there are several demining operations at work throughout the region, most of them international. But neither the Iraqi government nor the Kurdish government wants to give away, or take, responsibility. For the international operators, they cannot work without official government approval. But getting government approval from either side is very difficult, so at present, there is little we can do. My suggestion is that you apply to the Iraqi federal government."

I looked at the three of them, trying to hide my incredulity.

"Look," I said opening my laptop.

"These pictures were taken yesterday."

I clicked through a series of unexploded 155-howitzer rounds, mortar rounds, RPGs, and an assortment of homemade gas canister bombs and rockets.

"Who recovered these?" the international staff worker asked.

"The people, the children," I answered. "Can you at least give us some of the educational materials and send someone out to educate the people?"

The local manager looked at me and smiled professionally.

"Unfortunately, because of the situation, we are not able to provide any assistance to that area without approval first from the federal government in Baghdad, so as I said, you must apply there first."

"But the people are there now. They are coming to their homes. We cannot stop them," I said, attempting now to hold back anger.

"Well, you should perhaps tell them not to return until it is safe."

I looked over at the international staff person, who was frowning and looking down.

I checked myself and then spoke again.

"The people have been living in boxes for two years, waiting to return. We cannot stop them. I understand that we will have to wait for the demining. We understand that there is a war still going on. We understand that very well. We can hear it from the towns where we are working. But can you not just give us the educational materials? The posters, the pamphlets? I have seen the budget you have for this. What is the point of it if you cannot use it now when it is needed?"

"I am sorry, but you see our hands here are tied without approval from the government. All of these lands are disputed, and the situation is very complicated."

I was at a dead end with this man, and I knew it.

"Fine, thank you," I said, standing up. "I'll raise the issue with the US Mission in Baghdad tonight, and I'll prepare a brief for them of this conversation as well. You do understand, the donor countries support these budgets, believing this capability will actually be used?"

The local manager smiled and said he was quite sorry. Then the international staff member escorted me out of the office and out into the compound.

"Did you drive your own car here?" he asked once we were outside.

"Yes."

"See this door here?" he pointed.

"Yes."

"Bring your car here in one minute. Wait for me."

I got into the dusty Kia that was the community property of the priests and drove over to the door and waited. A minute later, he stepped out carrying three cardboard cases.

"The top one is in English, the bottom two in Arabic. Don't mention my name or tell anybody where these came from. But I am a Christian too, and I know what happened to your people."

He put the cases into the back of the car and disappeared. That night, we began distributing them in Batnaya and the other towns.

By April and Holy Week, the winter rains had stopped and the Nineveh Plain had been washed clean. Along the straight road that ran due south from Al-Qosh, through Teleskof and into Batnaya, on every side, the Biblical plain billowed in green with patches of yellow flowers under clear blue skies. It was difficult to believe that just two and a half years earlier, ISIS marauders had rampaged up this road, bringing a whirlwind of destruction and terror. The town of Batnaya still lay mostly in ruins, but the central roads had been plowed out and the main church structure of Mar Kyriakos was cleared and ready for the week to come.

Inside the sanctuary, the massive polished limestone pillars had been cleaned off and all the graffiti removed. All of the debris had been cleared from the foot of the destroyed altar, and a makeshift altar had been prepared in its place. Behind it stood a ten-foot-high cross with holders every six inches for votive candles.

In the religious processions that took place in the weeks and days ahead of Easter, hundreds of the town's residents drove in from surrounding areas, many from as far as Erbil, to participate. Moving slowly through the shattered town, surrounded by camouflaged security forces in body armor, weapons at the ready, the young and old sang and walked. Bishop Mikha, Fr. Salar, and the town elders at the head, the children running alongside, in and out of the processions, past the demolished buildings, past the twisted, burned-out trucks and cars, past the remains of the desecrated and looted cemetery, all around their town. Outside in the green fields, the birds, mostly sparrows, dove and swerved about in small flocks, their return a small sign of renewed life and encouragement.

On Easter Sunday, Mar Kyriakos was full even though the people could not yet permanently live in the town. Fr. Salar led the singing and chants of the deep and rich Chaldean liturgy, all in Aramaic, the ancient language of Christ. The deacons were dressed in white with floor-length robes and belts made of rope. White sashes hung about their necks as they gently swung the thurible. Slowly, the sanctuary filled with the haze of holy smoke and the smell of their ancestor's incense. I stood at the side of the sanctuary next to one of the town elders, who gently touched my arm and pointed to the ceiling high above where a tight grouping of bullet scars stood out. Then his arm moved down lower to a wide metal blade that came from a ceiling fan hanging twenty feet below the ceiling. The blade was shot through with half a dozen holes, and if you followed the trajectory, the source of the bullet scars on the ceiling became clear.

"Target practice," the elder said to me, shaking his head.

On the cross behind the makeshift altar, more than a hundred votive candles flickered. Later, as the communion lines neared an end, the Christian members of the security forces outside came forward in small groups, removing their helmets and carefully stacking their weapons as they entered the sanctuary. Hardened, dust-covered men in camouflage battle gear came forward to receive the sacraments from Fr. Aram, who moved close to the door to accommodate them. They had all stood together since the beginning of the crisis, and on that day, it seemed, they were truly coming home.

One week later, they had a feast celebrating their return to the town. The people of Batnaya gathered in a field along the perimeter road, pulling up their cars, spreading out blankets, tables, and chairs, sharing food and music, then gathering in circles to join in traditional dances. As the afternoon wore on, several trucks of Kurdish security forces pulled up along the perimeter road next to the field. The men climbed up onto the beds of the trucks, looking out at the celebration in front of them. These forces had initially been stationed in the area as part of the offensive in the fall, but their ongoing presence, months after the area had been cleared of ISIS, was now a source of growing anger for the Christians of Batnaya.

Much of the increasing hostility was a result of Christian allegations, most with hard evidence in support, that Kurdish forces were continuously, and openly, looting the homes of the Christians for anything of value since their arrival in November of 2016. Complaints to the Kurdish government in Erbil were met with assurances of dismay and denunciation of the practice, claiming it to be against their orders and procedures. At the same time, the government candidly admitted that in the present economic situation, where many members of the *Peshmerga* had gone for months without pay due to the impact of the war, there was little they could do to completely prevent the looting. The men had fought and shed blood to reclaim the region and believed they were justified in getting what they could for pay.

The Christians of Batnaya, and the region by then, held a different view. In their analysis, the Kurds, as a group, were not concerned about returning the Christian towns to their rightful ownership, regardless of the public statements of the government in Erbil. On the ground, the Christians sensed only that the Kurds, having fought as the main ground component against ISIS in the region, were now intending to claim the land as their own. In this environment, the open looting took on two foreboding aspects for the Christians.

First, it reinforced for the Christians what they historically experienced: disdain and lack of human respect towards them by the Kurds, often accompanied by violence. All Iraqi Christians over the age of thirty had memories of relatives who were alive at the time of the massacres in August of 1933. The Kurds were leading participants in a series of deadly pogroms that raged throughout the Christian towns and villages of northern Iraq. By some estimates, as many as 3,000 unarmed Christians, including women and children, were murdered in a frenzy of anti-Christian hysteria.[1]

Second, the Kurds insisted on keeping security control and a distinctly Kurdish military presence. They continued this highly visible presence over an area which war had long since passed through rather than turning control, even in part, over to the Christian soldiers and security personnel whose families had lived in these wholly Christian towns for more than a millennium. The Christians sensed a prelude to a larger plan in which the Kurds would gradually assume control of the lands and property and force out the Christians for good.

Meanwhile, outside Nineveh, the relations between Christians and Kurds were more nuanced. In Erbil, since the outset of the ISIS war, the leaders of the Kurdistan Regional Government had made legitimate public efforts to show solidarity with the Christians. During Christmas Day Mass in 2014 at St. Joseph's Church in Ankawa, the seat of the Chaldean archdiocese, Kurdish Prime Minister Nechirvan Barzani, was prominently seated in the front pew. The consensus among those in Erbil was that, in the current Barzani family leadership, the Christians mostly had friends, and in any case, they did not have antagonists. But the concern lay with what might come next in a change of government leadership. Christian residents of Erbil lived with daily forms of intimidation from average Kurds, so any form of trust regarding long-term treatment was thin and fragile.

In April 2017, the town elders from Batnaya looked hard at the Kurdish soldiers, who were watching and pointing at the Christian celebration below them. A group of Christian men, the fathers and husbands

---

[1] See: "IDC Remembers the Simele Massacre," *In Defense of Christians*, August 7, 2018, accessed October 2019, https://indefenseofchristians.org/idc-remembers-the-simele-massacre/; Marlo Safi, "The Simele Massacre & the Unsung Hero of the Genocide Convention," *National Review*, July 27, 2018, accessed October 2019, https://www.nationalreview.com /2018/07/simele-massacre-1933-assyrian-victims-still-seek-justice/.

of the women dancing together in circles in the field, approached the soldiers angrily, shouting at them to leave.

"This will not be good," said Fr. Salim, standing up and looking over to the brewing confrontation. "They must leave. This will not be good."

The men of the town were shouting loudly now, accusing the Kurds of watching the women. The town elders were out of their chairs as well and had moved toward the trucks. They stood there for several minutes, the Christians on the ground, arms moving angrily, some holding phones up to video the scene. The Kurds were standing on the trucks, looking down confidently. Eventually, having apparently made the calculation that leaving would ultimately be better than staying, the Kurds drove off. On the field, the wake of the confrontation washed up and over the hope that had been there twenty minutes before.

A town elder glowered at the scene and spoke aloud.

"This is our home. This is a Christian town. They should go."

* * *

As the gentle green warmth of spring evaporated into the blazing, parched inferno of the Iraqi summer, work in Batnaya slowed. While the larger focus remained on the grinding offensive in Mosul against the dwindling pocket of ISIS fighters who were holed up there, rebuilding the destroyed infrastructure of Batnaya remained a peripheral concern to those managing the large-scale relief efforts.

The Church continued its efforts, aided by small donations from around the world and scores of different volunteers, among them the startling presence of the young men and women of France serving through SOS Chrétiens d'Orient, a French Catholic non-government organization (NGO) dedicated to assisting the vulnerable Christians of the Middle East. SOS had been in Iraq since the beginning of the war, sending dozens of mostly college-aged men and women to care for the displaced and, later, aid in the restoration and recovery of the towns. The mission of the volunteers was only to serve. In Batnaya and neighboring Teleskof, their work crews were out daily, digging, hauling, painting, sweeping—whatever was asked of them. They would attend Mass as a group, dressed in their distinctive white T-shirts. No other country on earth, none, had sent their youth out to serve in Iraq this way. The joyous indifference of these young people to the harshness and potential danger of their surroundings was infectious, and the people of the towns grew to love many of them as their own.

Despite the lack of government and institutional aid support for the restoration of infrastructure in Batnaya, Thamir had persevered in the rebuilding of his home. By summer's end, he and his family had moved back in, nearly alone in the still-destroyed town, with only a handful of other families who had returned with him. They had solved the power problem, in part, by hacking into the power line supporting the Kurdish military compound just outside the town. Water was still being trucked in, but Thamir was in his home again, the first to come back and stay.

In early September, Fr. Salar and I went to Thamir's home to visit. Inside, the walls had all been patched and freshly painted. Family pictures were up, together with icons and other decorations. Newly refurbished furniture was put out in the living room, and a flat screen TV hung on the wall. Thamir's wife brought out tea, and the three young girls, all dressed in matching denim jumpsuits and silvered sneakers, stood in the next room, peeking around the corner. Thamir, wearing an old plaid flannel shirt and stained work jeans, led us around showing all the work he had done and what he planned to begin with next. As we all sat down, the girls came into the room, and the youngest sat down next to her father. I asked to take a family picture, and I have it in front of me now as I write these words. A family of five on their couch, back in their own home, shy smiles from the girls, a wary smile from their mother, and an undeniable look of pride and hope from Thamir.

That was early September. By the end of October, Thamir's wife and daughters were in Lebanon. Thamir followed them soon after, having given up. He said tearful goodbyes to all his friends, his house, and his town—now in the hands of the Shia-affiliated paramilitary unit known as the "Babylon Brigade," which was operating under its nominal Christian leader, Rayan al-Kildani. Despite the presence of its "Christian" leader, in reality, the Babylon Brigade was closely aligned with the Iranian-dominated Badr Organization, and its true allegiance lay there. In an article published in *The Huffington Post* on May 23, 2018, the sub-headline read: "The Babylon Brigade is led by a Christian but is tied to the brutal Iranian-backed Muslim paramilitary Badr Organization."[2]

What had happened? In perhaps the most monumental misjudgment in modern Kurdish history, Kurdish President Masoud Barzani had forced through an Independence Referendum for the Kurdistan Region from the federal government of Iraq on September 25, 2017. Pushing ahead with the referendum, against the public and private warning of its neighbors and Western allies, the referendum passed overwhelmingly in the polled areas of the Kurdistan Region. It gained over 90 percent of the collected vote and sent its supporters into a short-lived celebration of euphoric patriotism.

The truth of what lay behind Barzani's decision to press ahead remains obscure. Public and private diplomatic pressure from the US was clearly against the referendum at the time. The argument was that it would create a distraction from the heavy task still at hand for the coalition, namely finishing the war against ISIS. But it was also clear that many current and former US government officials, while they were not in the formal decision-making chain, had assured the Kurds that they had reliable friends in the US, despite the formal line being put forward by the officials in charge. Future scholars of US Mideast policy may eventually reveal the complete truth of what transpired in the months leading up to September 25th, but there remains no mystery as to what happened in its aftermath.

While the Kurdish government basked momentarily in its newly asserted pathway to independence, the Iraqi federal government in Baghdad mobilized. On October 15th, the Iraqi army advanced on Kirkuk in force. Within days, all across northern Iraq, territory that had been held by the Kurdish *Peshmerga* since 2014 or earlier was surrendered to the vastly superior numbers and firepower of the newly re-energized Iraqi army. There was little opposition from the Kurdish soldiers, who had been ordered to stand down. TV coverage showed the soldiers, many of whom had fought bravely against ISIS for years

---

2 See: Akbar Shahid Ahmed, "A Mostly Non-Christian Militia Won 2 of Iraqi Christians' Parliamentary Seats. Now Christians Want Trump To Intervene," *The Huffington Post*, May 23, 2018, accessed October 2019, https://www.huffpost.com/entry/iraq-parliament-christians -badr-organization_n_5b05dfd0e4b07c4ea104961f.

without pay and had lost friends and family in the conflict, now weeping bitterly in utter frustration and humiliation at the apparent weakness of the Kurdish response.

The Kurdish forces pulled back in Batnaya as well. The Babylon Brigade of the *Hashd Al-Sha'abi* paramilitary unit were filling in the vacuum as the *Peshmerga* drove out. Thamir, not waiting to see what fate would await his family under what appeared to be an Iranian-directed Shia militia, headed north with his family to Al-Qosh, to temporary safety.

But Al-Qosh was in a state of panic. Rumors had spread that the Kurds would be drawing back further. Al-Qosh, as well as everything south, would be turned over to the advancing Iraqi forces, as was represented by the Babylon Brigade. The Kurdish-affiliated local officials in Al-Qosh had packed up and fled the town. Most of the residents of Teleskof, north of Batnaya, which was only kilometers away from the Babylon Brigade forces by now, did the same. Only a platoon of Kurdish security was left behind in Teleskof, as well as a small group of the town's men and Fr. Salar, who had vowed to stay and protect the property of the town.

At first, it seemed that a peaceful agreement was being reached. The Kurds would withdraw from Al-Qosh and all the towns to the south. Iraqi federal security forces would come in to assume control of the towns, in place of the Babylon Brigade's paramilitary unit, whose presence was heavily opposed by nearly all the local Christians. The residents of Teleskof began to trickle cautiously back into the town. But as the days dragged on, the Kurdish forces stayed against the expectations of everyone, including the Americans whose maps had now shown that Teleskof had been turned over to the Iraqis.

Then on the night of October 22nd, shots were exchanged between the Iraqi forces, who had dug in just south of the town, and the Kurdish soldiers still garrisoned there. Mortar rounds landed inside the town, and two children were wounded. When the shooting subsided, the Iraqi commander made telephone contact with Fr. Salar and warned him to remove all the people from the town. If the Kurdish forces did not pull out by the next evening, the Iraqis would bombard the town using heavy artillery.

In an act of extraordinary defiance, Fr. Salar responded that he would send out the women and children, but that he would not leave, and neither would the group of men that were with him. If they were killed, it would be on hands of the Iraqis and the Kurds who chose to make a Christian town their place to fight amidst non-violent posturing that took place between the two groups at essentially every other contact point across northern Iraq.

Teleskof, at the time, held special significance as the only real place to which the displaced Christians had successfully returned. And almost none of that return had come as the result of aid from either the UN or the US. Instead, the success story of Teleskof came as the result of timely-delivered aid which came through a direct contract between the government of Hungary and the Chaldean Catholic Church. Throwing aside all common, Western, institutional, and governmental aid paradigms in use at the time, the Hungarians had made an assessment that the only legitimate civil group working in the region was the Church. And in the case of Teleskof, the Church was the only reliable partner. Following a policy which emphasized a specific preference for directly helping Christians who were victims of genocide, and a paradigm which sought to help people rebuild in their own countries rather than emigrate as strangers to a new land, the Hungarians granted the Church over two million euros in direct aid to support the recovery of Teleskof. The results were immediate. Bolstered with funds to work and a contractual framework which allowed for freedom in local decision-making, the town of Teleskof had recovered in a matter of months. The Hungarian approach, and the politics behind it, would become the subject of much controversy in the European Parliament and many other places. But for the people of Teleskof, all they knew was that they had been given a chance to rebuild their town and their lives, and they had taken it gratefully with both hands. They had succeeded, so it seemed, in scraping their life back from the abyss.

In full analysis, Teleskof had only been occupied by ISIS for a matter of weeks early on in the war. Then they made a strategic withdrawal back to lines just north of Batnaya. Other than their ritual traditional shooting up of the churches and small-scale looting of valuables,

Teleskof then remained largely abandoned and intact for the first years of the war, laying in between the dug-in front lines of the warring sides.

But the town was not completely unscathed. By May 3, 2016, coalition forces had pushed their forward front line just south of Teleskof. On that day, an ISIS force of more than 120 fighters smashed through the coalition lines using a battering ram of improvised commercial vehicles and bulldozers, welded with armor plating and crew-served weapons, and surprising a joint US and Kurdish advise-and-assist operation of less than two dozen men. A fourteen-hour battle ensued. A Navy Seal quick-reaction force, together with heavy air support from US F-15s, F-16s, A-10s, and B-52s, fought back and decimated the ISIS attackers, regaining control of the town. At the close of the battle, the buildings at the northern end of the town were shot through, and many of them flattened. Fifty-eight ISIS fighters were counted dead, and over twenty of their vehicles destroyed. "This was a large fight. There's no question about it," stated a US military spokesman.[3]

The battle was not without its costs for the coalition forces. At 9:32 a.m., Special Warfare Operator 1st Class Charles "Chuck" Keating IV, thirty-one years old from San Diego, California, was struck and killed just north of the town by a direct hit from ISIS. The US spokesman said of Keating's death, "He was killed by direct fire. This was a gunfight, so there were bullets everywhere."

In the months that followed, and into the new year, then on into the fall of 2017, Fr. Salar and I would often pass the spot alongside the road where Charlie Keating gave his life. We would speak about what it would mean for history to understand and remember that, despite everything that had gone wrong, the Americans had come back, and died there, in order to save this town. We hoped that someday, when stability was fully returned, that we could put together some type of remembrance of all that had taken place there during the war years, something that would provide some sense of healing and closure for all those who had been affected.

---

[3] Sam LaGrone, "U.S. Officials Describe Fight That Killed Navy SEAL Charles Keating IV," *USNI News*, May 4, 2016, accessed October 2019, https://news.usni.org/2016/05/04/u-s -officials-describe-fight-that-killed-navy-seal-charles-keating-iv.

Photo by Stephen M. Rasche

Fr. Salar Kajo, Chaldean Catholic priest of Teleskof, Nineveh Plain, Northern Iraq, standing above his recovered town in April, 2017. In October of that year, he would risk his life to defy both Kurdish and Iraqi forces who were poised to make his rebuilt town a battlefield. Just outside the town, US Navy Seal Charlie Keating had been killed in a heavy battle with ISIS fighters in May, 2016.

All of this truth lay beneath Fr. Salar's words when we spoke by phone on October 23, 2017. I was in Belgium then, staying with the Lebanese Maronite fathers at their abbey outside Brussels, preparing for meetings with the EU Parliament before returning to Iraq.

"I will not go," he said to me. "My people will not go either. We have rebuilt this town without any help from the Iraqi government. Now they threaten us. They will destroy us? People have made sacrifices here, Stephen, many people. You know this."

"What are the Kurds doing?" I asked.

"They are taking over the homes and setting up inside them with their weapons. I have told them they cannot do this. They are making targets of our homes. I have told them if they want to fight with the Iraqis, fine, okay, but go and do it somewhere else. This town is not yours to destroy again."

Photo by Stephen M. Rasche

Thamir and his family upon their return to their family home in Batnaya, September, 2017, after three years of living as displaced persons due to the ISIS war. One month later, they would all be refugees in Lebanon, having been forced from their home by Iraqi-Kurdish conflict and the arrival of Iranian-backed *Hashd Al Shaabi* units into the town.

In the following twenty-four hours, together with our closest partners, we worked the phones calling all our friends and supporters in Iraq, Europe, and the US. The US National Security Council personnel, responsible for Iraq, fully understood the implications of an Iraqi attack on Teleskof. They also understood the issue of the Kurds deciding to make their stand on Christian land—to which they held no rightful historical claim—while having pulled back from areas of legitimate Kurdish claims, seemingly without a struggle. From our side, we made it clear that if there was renewed fighting with Christian casualties or destruction of homes in Teleskof, that it would likely mean the end for any other Christian attempts to return anywhere in Nineveh. In Baghdad, US Ambassador Silliman set up an open line with Fr. Salar in Teleskof to monitor the situation. Over the coming days, under heavy US pressure and diplomacy, both the Kurds and Iraqis backed down, struck an uneasy truce, and dug in on either side of a new line, now running east to west between the towns of Batnaya and Teleskof.

A week later, Thamir ventured back to Batnaya. The doors of his home had been smashed open, everything inside looted. He complained to the Iraqi army officers, who blamed the Kurds. Meanwhile, lurking about the town, he saw the members of the Babylon Brigade—none of them Christian—walking about casually with their Kalashnikovs slung loosely over their shoulders. Thamir drove back up the road to the north. He packed up his wife and daughters and sent them to stay with friends in Lebanon. A few weeks later, he joined them there, and together they registered as refugees. They entered the diaspora, hoping that, someday in the future, they would join the rest of his family in Australia.

Months later, Thamir spoke with Fr. Salar by phone. Things were not easy in Lebanon. He was out of money, he had no work, Australia was closed for new refugees, his daughters were growing up, and he was worried about his future.

"Come back here," Fr. Salar told him. "We can find you work somewhere; you can rebuild here in Teleskof or another place. Maybe Batnaya will still come back to us."

But there was no convincing him anymore. He had lost hope in Iraq, he said. There was no solution for the Christians there. Staying in Iraq, doing all of that work, he had just lost time for himself and his wife and his daughters. He should have listened to his family in Australia and gone when there was still a chance. He should have listened to them, he said. They were right.

CHAPTER 4

The Help That Came

"You have to understand, our government is broken." I was speaking to a USAID official at a conference in Washington, DC, who was nearing retirement and had lived to see the changes that had occurred over the last three decades at his agency.

"Process is our friend here. If you follow the process, you will always be safe. The outcome is never primary, especially in a long-term project, because chances are, you will have been transferred into a new assignment before anything gets finished. So you just want to make sure you have followed process."

In the years since the outset of the ISIS war, those of us inside the Church had come up against this mentality time and again whenever we tried to integrate assistance from the US or EU into the work we had been doing. In retrospect, perhaps the disconnect in purpose was simply too great.

For the Church, we were focused on service, and that was our vocation. Our only measurement was in the number of families and persons we served and kept intact. We were not seeking additional compensation or career advancement, but only to address the crisis in front of us. For the government agencies in the US and EU, the issue of dealing with any crisis was inevitably intertwined with the ways in which any assistance furthered larger policy goals and supported the continuing funding needs of the agency involved. But for us, the needy were at our door.

Still, the possibility of major government assistance seemed, to us, the best long-term solution, or at least a large part of it. Beginning in the fall of 2014 and throughout the dark years of 2015 and 2016, the Church in Iraq had met the needs of over 100,000 displaced Christians, and many displaced Muslim and Yazidis, without any government or institutional help. But this was not sustainable, especially since there was no end to the conflict in sight. As a church, not an institutional aid organization, we did not fit into the system for government aid grants. Still, there was ready acknowledgement from all, including those at the UN mission, that we had been the primary provider for the past two years, and had done so at a level which, in many ways, exceeded the UN standards.

How did the Church, in its pastoral and spiritual role, end up as a major provider of humanitarian aid, seemingly overnight? This had not been planned, but instead evolved out of the crisis as it unfolded.

As the ISIS tide rose throughout northern Iraq in 2014, the US and the global community, including the UN mission in Erbil, had long since been in the process of drawing down. In August of 2010, President Obama officially declared that the "American combat mission has ended. Operation Iraqi Freedom is over, and the Iraqi people now have lead responsibility for the security of their country."[1] That same month, the last US combat brigade, the 4th Stryker Brigade of the 2nd Infantry Division out of Fort Carson, Colorado, headed home. By December of 2011, the few remaining US troops that had stayed for training and security assistance had left Iraq as well. The country and its military were on their own.

With stunning speed and violence, ISIS swept through northern and western Iraq in the summer of 2014, and nobody was prepared. Iraqi and Kurdish troops alike fled from the towns of the Nineveh Plain, east

---

[1] Office of the Press Secretary, The White House, "Remarks by the President in Address to the Nation on the End of Combat Operations in Iraq," August 31, 2010, https:// obamawhitehouse.archives.gov/the-press-office/2010/08/31/remarks-president-address -nation-end-combat-operations-iraq.

of Mosul, pausing barely, if at all, to warn the townspeople they had promised to protect. A mass exodus of panic-stricken civilians, including over 100,000 Christians, followed on their heels. By August 7th, ISIS fighters had taken Makhmour, only twenty miles from the Kurdish capital of Erbil. The arrival of US air support on August 8th under operation *Inherent Resolve* halted the ISIS advance just outside the city, but the flood of displaced families into Erbil from throughout the region continued without stop for weeks.

Farther south in Baghdad, the federal government was already engaged in a furious battle of its own against ISIS elements. By June, ISIS had reached a point only sixty miles north of the city. Having lost control of nearly the entire western half of the country, its army having, in many cases, simply evaporated before the enemy, the central government was in its own state of paralysis. They focused on coordinating the rapidly arming pro-government militias who would shoulder much of the fight to come. The issue of how to handle displaced people in the north was beyond their capacity now, in every way.

Meanwhile in Erbil, the masses arrived in the city, beginning with tens of thousands in the three days of August 6-8. In most cases, those arriving had only minutes to prepare themselves before they fled their homes in Nineveh. Later, the displaced civilians would claim that the Kurdish security forces had fled from the towns ahead of the bewildered people, many of whom were fast asleep, giving only the barest of warnings that ISIS fighters were on their way and just down the road. In a matter that would cement an element of permanent distrust, the Kurdish security forces then left the civilians behind to fend for themselves. Just weeks before, these same security forces had disarmed the civilians of Nineveh on the basis that the Kurdish presence negated any need for private arms. For the people, the panicked departure of the Kurds would be the second time that summer that the security forces allegedly in place to protect them had fled. In the aftermath of the fall of Mosul in June, the Iraqi security forces had fled from much of the rest of Nineveh as well, and it was into this void that the Kurdish forces had temporarily arrived, only to then flee themselves.

Disarmed and without protection, the terrified people gathered everything of importance they could into their cars and trucks, and joined a fleeing mass heading east, towards the first checkpoints, into the Kurdistan Region. There, they met with further depredations. The truth of what transpired at the checkpoints remains a matter of dispute. From the Kurdish side, their security forces were overwhelmed with the sheer number of panic-stricken people and had legitimate fears that ISIS members were infiltrating the moving crowd. Perhaps, the Kurds reasoned, ISIS had cars already rigged with explosives set to go off once they entered the city of Erbil. The only way to ensure protection was to confiscate the vehicles and let the people proceed by foot. Recollections from the displaced families tell a different story. They claim the security concerns were just a pretext to loot them further and seize their cars for profit.

Whatever the truth was, the displaced arrived in Erbil in the coming days on foot, mostly just wearing the clothes they had. They had walked dozens of miles through the blazing Iraqi summer. And for the Christians, they went to the one place where they knew they would be taken in—the churches.

* * *

"It was like a flood," the archbishop of Erbil, Bashar Warda, would later say. "Like a biblical flood. First, you heard the rise of noise. Then the first few showed. And then, almost at once, the streets were filled, and it was like a sea, a sea of people washed up from the desert."

Ankawa, the Christian enclave in Erbil where his archdiocese held seat, had an existing population of 30,000 people. Within the first twenty-four hours of the incoming flood of distraught and exhausted people, that number would swell to over 100,000.

"For some, especially the elderly, they were as ghosts," he continued. "For them, we just wanted to put them into the shade and give them water before they died, and many of them were close to it, I am sure. In the women, you could see the fear for their children, and in the children themselves, you could see the confusion of it all. But in the men, there was no doubt, there was anger in their eyes. They had just lost everything, really everything, and they knew they had been betrayed by someone.

"Our people from the town, all of them came out to help these people. We put them first in all the church buildings. In the sanctuaries, they laid down on the pews and everywhere on the floors. When the buildings were full, we put them on the grass outside. We found tents and tarps and used everything we could find to give them some shelter. In the night, we cooked up food inside the church compound and fed everyone who came. But when I finally went to my room to lie down, I could not sleep. Just meters away, just outside my window, were thousands of these poor people with no place to go. I could not just leave them on the ground. But what could we do? I prayed to God, please dear Lord, show me, what can I do?"

In the days that followed, it was not only the Church and its leaders that struggled for an answer to the human tidal wave that struck Erbil. The Kurdistan Regional Government (KRG) itself was overwhelmed to the point of paralysis, for it was not only Christians that had fled the ISIS wave of terror, but hundreds of thousands of Muslims and Yazidis as well. The UN mission was working to turn its ship around and regroup, but it was a slow-moving process. At the time, they were too understaffed and underfunded to deal with what was soon becoming the largest concentration of displaced persons on earth. In the breach, a deal was struck between the leaders of the KRG and the heads of the Christian churches: the KRG would provide land and basic security for the Christians, and the churches would be responsible for providing their people with everything else—food, housing, medicine, education—everything. In exchange, the KRG would agree to otherwise let the Christians manage their own fate. And with this understanding in place, the Chaldean Catholic Archdiocese of Erbil, together with the displaced diocese leaders from the Syriac Catholic and Orthodox churches of Mosul and Nineveh, became full-time humanitarian aid workers. While most of them thought this emergency service would be of short duration, others shook their heads, knowing something different.

Chaldean Fr. Douglas Bazi, himself displaced from Baghdad to Erbil years earlier after having been kidnapped for ransom by a Shia criminal gang in 2006 and tortured for six days before his release, looked at the scene and knew this would not be over soon. He thought these people would be there for years and prayed for faith to see to the end.

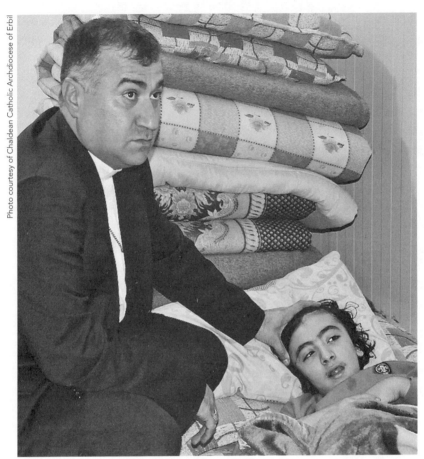

Photo courtesy of Chaldean Catholic Archdiocese of Erbil

Archbishop Bashar Warda of Erbil tends to a displaced Christian child from Nineveh, Northern Iraq, in an emergency shelter provided by the Archdiocese after ISIS attacks, August, 2014.

While the churches and their small staff may have been long on faith, they were short on nearly everything else. The most pressing, immediate needs were food and housing. As it was still summer, with daily temperatures well above one hundred degrees Fahrenheit, the churches began to move families into cooler shelter in the many unfinished building skeletons throughout Ankawa. There, inside these empty cement spaces, local engineers had thrown up makeshift walls, which were often no more than tarps tied up to roped grids. Temporary water lines were run into the buildings and portable toilets installed outside. Food kitchens were set up throughout the city, and gradually, the people were moved from outside tents and church room floors into the shelters.

Meanwhile, around the world, television viewers watched in horror as the deepening crisis marauded its way across the screens in front of them. The thriving Chaldean immigrant communities in Michigan and Southern California, many of whose families were first- or second-generation immigrants from the very towns that had been overrun by ISIS, were hearing directly by phone from their family and friends who were now homeless in Erbil. The churches were also hearing from their related congregations and conferences around the world. And soon, the same instant media coverage of the crisis which had horrified the outside world as viewers now motivated them as actors.

In Europe, the Catholic aid organization known as *Kirche in Not* at its headquarters in Germany, and *Aid to the Church in Need* (ACN) elsewhere in the world, stepped forward immediately and began drawing on its global network to provide funds. Over the course of the next three years, ACN would become the leading donor to the humanitarian aid programs run by the archdiocese. Later, when the return to Nineveh came into view, ACN would be the founding donor for the establishment of the Nineveh Reconstruction Committee. Also from Germany came donations from Missio Aachen and the Diocese of Rottenburg-Stuttgart, as well as the Italian Bishop's Conference and Caritas Italy. From France came support from L'Oeuvre D'Orient and Chrétiens D'Orient. And from the US arrived help from the Chaldean community, the Knights of Columbus, and ACN USA. Working primarily within the Yazidi community but also providing substantial support to the Christians, Samaritan's Purse and other Evangelical aid organizations soon arrived as well. Altogether, by 2017, there would be nearly four dozen separate private donors, nearly all of them faith-based. Throughout the crisis, this private, largely Christian, international network provided the base of support through which the local churches in northern Iraq took care of the displaced for the next three years.

In time, the relationship with the Knights of Columbus would prove to be of historical importance to the effort and, in many key ways, perhaps began paving the way for a new paradigm of aid delivery. As

ISIS smashed its way through Iraq, the Knights made an enormous contribution to the Christian community living there, both in terms of material assistance and advocacy. Almost as soon as ISIS overran Mosul, the Knights' CEO, Carl Anderson, made the issue a top priority for their nearly two-million-person strong Catholic organization.

By the end of 2014, the Knights of Columbus had contributed $2.6 million for Christians and those in their care who were displaced in Iraq and Syria. Five years later, their commitment had topped $25 million. The funds raised by the Knights of Columbus helped support numerous projects for those in Iraq, Syria, and Egypt, as well as for Christians who had fled to Lebanon, Jordan, and the United States.

In Iraq, the Knights supported projects for the Archdiocese of Erbil, including education classes, food distribution to displaced families, and rental subsidies. They also built an apartment building with 140 units designed to be the new home for displaced Christians who could not return to their cities and villages. The apartment complex was named "McGivney House" for the Knights of Columbus' founder, the Venerable Fr. Michael McGivney.

The Knights also took on the enormous task of funding the rebuilding of the town of Karemlesh. Following on the success of the Hungarian model used to rebuild Teleskof, in 2017, the Knights committed $2 million directly to the Church for the rebuilding of Karemlesh, and within months, the town sprang back to life as hundreds of families were able to move back home.

It was not just the Chaldean Archdiocese of Erbil that received support from the Knights. The Melkite archbishop of Aleppo, Syria, received substantial humanitarian help, as did the Syriac priests who were displaced from Mosul and Nineveh. The Knights also committed to helping rebuild the Syriac Cathedral in Baghdede, also known as Qaraqosh, the largest Christian town in Nineveh. They pledged support to the Syriac Church in the United States, whose diaspora community included an influx of refugees from ISIS and whose territory covered the entire country. The Knights also supported the work of Syriac Catholic Patriarchate for refugees, primarily in Lebanon.

In addition, health clinics in Erbil and Duhok, run by the St. Elizabeth College of Health and Social Work in Bratislava, received substantial funding from the Knights. The Duhok clinic in particular was vital, as it was often the first medical stop for Yazidi women who had been sexually enslaved by ISIS.

In Egypt, the Coptic Orthodox Church received support from the Knights after the bombings of their churches in that country, and support was also provided for educational programs in Jordan for those displaced from Iraq and Syria by ISIS.

It wasn't just the level of aid that set the efforts of Knights apart. The organization was also an enormous help in raising awareness about the issues confronting Christian and other minority communities in Iraq and Syria. Without the leadership of the Knights of Columbus, it is virtually certain that Secretary of State John Kerry would never have declared ISIS's actions against Christians, Yazidis, and Shia Muslims as constituting genocide.

The Kerry State Department had been obligated by Congress to declare by March 17, 2016, as to whether ISIS's actions had risen to the level of genocide. By all indications, they were disinclined to do so, especially with regard to the targeted Christian communities. Whether the lack of desire to take up the issue was driven by politics or inertia is unclear, but the opposition to making the designation was strong.

One public report had profiled the Yazidis' plight, but no similar report had been done for the Christians. Informed, off-the-record comments coming from the State Department indicated that perhaps a genocide designation would be made—but that Christians would likely not be included. Some in the State Department seemed sympathetic to what the Christian community had suffered under ISIS, and one senior official told the Knights that if the organization believed this was genocide, then they should try to prove it since the State Department was not in a position to do so.

Though they had only about a month to make the case, the Knights set to work, even sending an attorney—Scott Lloyd—to Iraq to stay with the Archdiocese of Erbil and do witness interviews. Meanwhile in the United States, the Knights worked with Chaldean, Syriac, and Melkite bishops and expatriate members of Middle Eastern Christian communities to get a clear sense of what had happened on the ground. The Knights were able to tap into the Catholic Church's network in which information was flowing up from parishioners to priests to bishops, with the latter then able to provide an overall view of the situation.

From this effort the Knights created a report—assisted by the group In Defense of Christians—and collected additional reports from other organizations in Iraq, Europe, and the United States that had documented ISIS's atrocities against the Christian community. The nearly 300-page final report included a thorough legal analysis by Professor Robert Destro of the Catholic University of America as to why the acts of ISIS justified the designation of genocide.[2] It also included lists of Christians killed and churches bombed, as well as a copy of ISIS's sex slave price list for Christian and Yazidi women.

The evidence was overwhelming. So was the public awareness and media effort. More than 100,000 people signed the Knights' petition urging Kerry to make the designation. The Knights also aired commercials calling for a genocide declaration and were interviewed by major news outlets around the country on the issue.

The March 10 press conference unveiling the genocide report included a Chaldean priest who had been kidnapped and tortured by Islamist terrorists in Baghdad—Fr. Douglas Bazi. It also included Coptic Archbishop Angaelos of London, whose community had been targeted by ISIS in the infamous beheadings on the Libyan beach.

The evidence, combined with the public pressure, had an effect. ISIS was committing genocide; this was first stated clearly by Congress—unanimously with the passage of H. Con. Res. 75—and then a few days later with Secretary Kerry's statement on the morning of March 17, 2016.

The words were important, but the genocide-targeted communities still were being overlooked by US government and UN funding. The Knights spoke out about this publicly, regularly urging action in op-eds and in the media, both before and after the 2016 election.

---

2 On September 23, 2019, Destro was appointed as Assistant Secretary of State, Bureau of Democracy, Human Rights, and Labor. Ironically, this was the same post held under the Obama Administration by Tom Malinowksi, who had earlier told the assembled Christian bishops of Northern Iraq that no genocide declaration would be forthcoming as discussed in detail supra pp. 48-50.

The case they were making gained traction in 2017, especially as more and more ISIS-held minority towns were liberated. Some in the Obama administration had relied on the Knights to "prove" the case for genocide, and during the Trump administration, the Knights—as producers of the genocide report and a high profile public voice with solid connections with Christian and Yazidi leaders—again found themselves relied upon for insight into the post-genocide situation in Iraq.

USAID entered into an MOU with the Knights to share information and work jointly on projects in Iraq, and they were frequently consulted by USAID and other agencies as issues arose that related to genocide-targeted communities.

On the legislative side as well, the Knights had an impact. H.R. 390, the Iraq and Syria Genocide Relief and Accountability Act, was based in part on the testimony of Knights' CEO Carl Anderson. It would pass both the House and Senate unanimously and be signed into law by President Trump in late 2018 at a ceremony at the White House, attended by Archbishop Warda.

When a delegation from the Knights, headed by Carl Anderson, visited Iraq in early 2019, they met many there, including bishops and priests. Again and again, they heard the following from the Christian leaders about how critical the assistance of the Knights had been to their survival. In addition to the $25 million the Knights had committed and its effective advocacy for the targeted communities, the Catholic organization had been a uniquely good partner. As a mission driven charitable organization, the Knights took no overhead costs from the money they raised on behalf of the persecuted and displaced. And they listened. The Knights didn't impose their view of what needed to happen but worked to meet the needs of the people and did all they could to make the experience of the aid recipients as simple as possible. In many ways, their assistance was a model for how humanitarian aid and reconstruction can work when an aid organization puts its money to work directly with the local entities who are in the best position to assist the displaced. In the hyper-partisan world of Washington politics which followed the arrival of the Trump administration, the Knights would find themselves repeatedly in the spotlight. In the view of some, the faith based nature of the Knights work made them immediately suspect.[3] But for the displaced minorities of Iraq, both Christian and Yazidi alike, they only knew that the symbol of the Knights meant that significant and honest help was being sent to them directly from a group of American people who cared.

[3] See: Felicia Sonmez, "Hawaii Rep. Tulsi Gabbard accuses fellow Democrats of 'religious bigotry' in questioning judicial nominee," *Washington Post*, Jan. 10, 2019, accessed October, 2019, https://www.washingtonpost.com/politics/hawaii-rep-tulsi-gabbard-accuses-fellow-democrats-of-religious-bigotry-in-questioning-judicial-nominee/2019/01/09/2c17ecdc-1467-11e9-90a8-136fa44b80ba_story.html.

CHAPTER 5

From America

It was December of 2016. Congressman Chris Smith and his accompanying staff would be arriving in Erbil the next week. The trip came as a follow-up to our earlier testimony before his committee in September. The Obama State Department, still in power ahead of the inauguration, had given little help or encouragement to the visit. Smith had been a constant critic of the Obama administration's policy as it pertained to the persecuted minorities of Iraq, and there was little reason to expect that Smith's visit was going to uncover additional information that would change any of this criticism.

But Smith was undeterred. In their careers in Congress, he and former colleague Frank Wolf had traveled the world, getting their own firsthand view of the situation in conflict zones, especially where minorities were being threatened and persecuted. Despite multiple attempts to stall the trip by the State Department, Smith pressed on with the leverage at his disposal, and the trip was ultimately a go. The trip would have a narrow and focused purpose, and that was to meet directly with genocide survivors and to visit with the Archdiocese of Erbil and meet directly with the people who were managing the humanitarian aid efforts on the ground for the displaced Christians and Yazidis.

Once the dates had been fixed, we set about preparing the itinerary. While most of the meetings would take place inside the rectory compound, where we could bring in the different visitors to speak directly with the Congressman and his staff, it was also important for him to also see firsthand the living situation for the displaced families. We agreed that the best place for this on a short visit would be the Ashti II camp run by Fr. Emmanuel of the Syriac Catholic Church. At the time, there were nearly 8,000 displaced Christians living there, all in one camp.

In preparing for the visit, it was necessary for the State Department resident security team to come out and assess the site. I was their guide around the camp and introduced them to Fr. Emmanuel. Accompanying them was a young woman from the consulate whose position was coordinator for IDP programs. We had only met by phone in the last few days, and this would be our first meeting in person. Prior to this, we had never been advised that an IDP coordinator position existed.

When the small convoy of armored Chevrolet Suburbans arrived into the Ashti II compound, Fr. Emmanuel and I directed them in for parking. Then we welcomed the IDP coordinator and two members of the security team inside Fr. Emmanuel's trailer office, the rest of the bearded Americans taking up positions outside. After mutual introductions and serving of tea, Fr. Emmanuel spoke, a smile on his face and his hands held apart, palms upward, in welcome.

"I welcome you here to the Ashti camp, the largest Christian camp in Ankawa. In the two years that we have been here, you are the first person from the American government to come and visit us."

The US coordinator looked over at me, then back to Fr. Emmanuel.

"But you have a UN coordinator office here?" she asked, searchingly.

Fr. Emmanuel smiled and laughed softly.

"We have no UN coordinator office here. The UN never comes here. In the first days, they came with some tarps, which, of course, we were very pleased to receive. They are very good tarps, and you can see them on all the homes. But they do not come here since this time."

"But who is supporting this camp?" the coordinator asked.

Fr. Emmanuel looked at me, not sure how to answer, and I stepped in.

"This camp is run by the Church. The UN is not involved here at all. The shelters have come through private organizations, and the

Church coordinates it all. The schools that are here for the children, the safety and security of the people, all of it is run through the Church. Fr. Emmanuel is not just the priest here; he is also like a small-town mayor."

"And he does this all himself?" she asked.

"No," I answered. "There are other priests here and also town elders. It is a very complete community in that sense."

"But do you take part in the UN cluster group meetings?" she asked.

"Well," I answered, "we are not an official NGO. We are just the Church. The cluster group is for NGOs, and we are not registered or certified for this. Last year, we spoke with the UN about it, and they advised that we could be observers if we wished, but honestly, they were not encouraging about it. Perhaps we should have persevered, but as you can see here, we have our hands full, and our staff is very small. In any case, we had already been told by senior management for the UN, both here and in Washington, DC, that our situation would not qualify for help unless we wanted to just send the people to the UN camps, and they will not go there because they are afraid for their safety."

Then we all stepped outside and brought them around the vast camp. As we walked, I spoke with the coordinator, and it was clear that she was bewildered, unsure of how to react. Here was a town of displaced Christians, operating by themselves for more than two years, not over a mile and a half away from the US consulate and the UN compound, and the US and the UN had zero vision as to what was taking place there.

In truth, I felt for her. It was clear she was concerned and wanted to help. But like so many of her colleagues, she was boxed in by the security and duty policies being used there in Iraq. From the security standpoint, the consular staff lived in virtual isolation from the city of Erbil and the life around them. Any forays outside the blast walls needed to be planned days or, more often, weeks in advance, with every part of the move coordinated and planned. Interactions the staff had with locals came only through carefully staged meetings and official social gatherings within heavily secured buildings. There, the captive US staff would hear, from the local authorities and officials, a well-scripted version of the situation outside the walls.

In contrast, with the exception of the British, who were equally restrictive of their personnel, most other consular offices allowed their staff to have relative freedom in mixing with the locals. But for the Americans, sealed off as they were, you could not help but question how effective they could actually be in their judgments and assessments of the situation. It was a difficult question, and clearly the Americans posed a much different kind of target than other countries due to their legions of sworn enemies among the various Middle Eastern militias and terror organizations. At the same time, the security paradigm itself was perhaps the greatest inhibitor to the consular staff from doing substantively informed work. In a real sense, the security considerations and prohibitions effectively negated the presence and the work itself. From there, one came quickly to question as to what the actual need was for much of the staff to be permanently stationed there in Iraq, as opposed to being given a desk back in the US and three trips a year to the site country.

The situation was further impacted by the fact that Iraq was structured as a one-year duty station due to the hardship of the location. Again, the reality of the Iraq station was inescapable, and family dependents were not sent, thereby placing great strain on the consular and embassy staff. At the same time, Iraq was directly centered on multiple strategic and political fault lines of enormous national security implications for the US, and its realities and ways were among the most complex on earth. By the time new staff arrived and began to understand the actual workings of things and establish even basic rapport with others outside their compounds, their duty tour was up, and they would move on, the files handed over to the next team, who would start the process all over again.

In my years in Iraq, I would discuss this situation repeatedly with career Foreign Service employees, most of whom expressed sincere frustration themselves at these obstacles that stood in their way. Not infrequently, I was asked by these same employees to make a complaint about the issue, about how the security and duty paradigms were in themselves posing a security risk to the US by preventing them from doing their jobs. Clearly the fault here lay not with the mission-oriented security teams themselves, who had a job to do, and who did it as well as any group on earth. But at some point, for the work there in Iraq, the proper trade-off between security and meaningful presence was increasingly blurred.

The irony of all of the security constraints was brought into even sharper focus when Congressman Smith arrived in Erbil several days later. With the State Department still pushing back on the delegation even as it landed in Erbil, the trip out to the Ashti II camp was in jeopardy due to perceived security threats. While the congressman met with various members of the displaced community within the safety of the rectory compound, his aides continued negotiating with the local consular staff regarding approval for the visit outside to the Ashti camp. After several hours, with the day winding down and the window of opportunity closing, Smith took the matter into his own hands, waiving the request for State Department security and taking individual responsibility for his safety. As part of the arrangement, rather than US State Department security, the congressman would be accompanied by two truckloads of Kurdish security forces. His delegation could include only himself and his chief of staff, along with two representatives from the archdiocese who would drive the congressman directly to the camp in one of our cars. With that, Archbishop Warda pointed at me and said, "You will come, and I will drive. We will take my car."

Smith clapped his hands together, looked at his chief of staff, and said, "Let's go."

So off we went, the archbishop driving, Congressman Smith in the front seat with him, and me and Mark Milosch, then Chief of Staff for the US Helsinki Commission,[1] in the back. Meanwhile, clearing the road out front, roared a Kurdish security truck with eight heavily-armed men sitting in the back, ready to jump out at a moment's notice. Following closely behind was a similar truck. In only a few minutes, we arrived at the camp.

Welcoming us in was Fr. Emmanuel, who showed the congressman a map of his compound and described the situation there. Then the tour proceeded around the camp, with Smith being invited into the cramped housing units by family after family, eventually ending up at the community center next to the church, which formed the nucleus of the camp. All the while, the Kurdish security forces had respectfully

---

[1] The US Helsinki Commission is a US government commission that promotes human rights, military security, and economic cooperation in Europe, Eurasia and North America, https://www.csce.gov.

laid back and away from our delegation, letting the congressman mingle freely. Inside the community center, the room was packed with young children practicing Christmas songs ahead of the coming week of celebrations. The conductor invited the congressman up to the front of the room, where he gave them a Christmas greeting from their friends in the US.

With that, we headed back to the archbishop's Toyota and drove back to the church compound, the Kurdish security trucks coming to a screeching halt in front of the driveway gate. Smiling and waving at us we got out, they drove away.

Later that night, the word of an important American visiting from Washington, DC, rippled through the Ashti II camp. Nobody from the US had ever visited with them before, and his presence there, mixing directly with the people, without ceremony or fear, had a profound impact on them. If, they thought, this American can come in here and be with us like this, maybe there actually is hope for us.

From a professional security standpoint, there is no doubt the visit would have been judged a nightmare. But from a goodwill and foreign policy standpoint, it was priceless. What the Iraqis, including the Christians, had come to know about US government officials was that when they showed up, everybody else should be afraid. Clearly that method had its purpose, especially in Iraq, where the hidden danger was undeniable and ever present. At the same time, the US had taken it upon itself to come into this country, and our role in creating the chaos and horror that ravaged Iraq was equally undeniable. Where was the bridge we would ever cross to get past it? Did it even exist? There is still much history yet to come before that answer becomes clear, but on that December day, there was no doubt in my mind that Chris Smith had shown the face of American solidarity that the displaced Christians in Ashti II needed to see.

Surprisingly, or perhaps not, two days after the visit of the IDP coordinator from the US consulate, and just a day before the arrival of the Smith delegation, a container truck filled with boxes marked with UNICEF logos pulled into the Ashti II camp. They were accompanied by a group of workers wearing jackets with emblems of a local NGO, who was working as an implementer for the UN. The boxes were filled with winter jackets for children and blankets, and the NGO crew was handing out these boxes to the people of the camp. I asked Fr. Emmanuel if he knew about it, and he said no. They had just showed up. I asked if he had ever seen them come in before.

He smiled and looked at me. "In this week, we have seen many things for the first time."

* * *

DESPITE THE VITAL HELP OF THE KNIGHTS, ACN, and others, as the crisis moved into 2016 and its second year, money was running out and the strain of displacement was taking its toll out in the larger Christian camps. While the Church standards were above those being delivered by the UN to other displaced people, they were hardly conditions that could be held under control for much longer without improvement and additional support. We were trying to give them hope to stay in Iraq, and they needed something beyond bare subsistence in order to hang on. In one camp, over a thousand people were packed into shoddy makeshift "caravan" shelters. They had been living for over a year in the former grounds of a youth sports center, and now tempers and cooperation were reaching their breaking point. The Syriac Catholic priest assigned for the management of the camp had been angrily cornered by some of the inhabitants in late May. Increasing water and power shortages were creating daily conflicts. If we were going to lose control of the situation, it would begin there, and Archbishop Warda knew it. These people needed to be moved out, said the archbishop. That was our top priority.

By then, we had been in ongoing discussions for several months with the Nazarene Fund, a faith-based non-profit effort out of Texas that received the bulk of its funding through the efforts of Glenn Beck and his Mercury One organization. Formed at the outset of the ISIS war, the leaders of the Nazarene Fund had been searching for ways to effectively engage in the effort to support the displaced Christians of Nineveh. Working closely together with their logistics chief, a mission-focused ex-Marine who later found himself a place in the Trump State Department, we drew up a plan to remove the inhabitants from the sports center camp. They'd be placed into group homes—three and four families to a home—with working bathrooms and showers. Erbil, at that time, had thousands of empty apartments, many of them new and never yet inhabited. Their use had been halted by the demise of the economy and the departure of people due to the war. Using the position of the archdiocese to bargain for apartment leases, backed by the support of the Nazarene fund, on June 6, 2016, we began to clear the camp.

The management of the transfer had been given to Deacon Shwan of the Chaldean archdiocese and me. At first, the people were suspicious and could not believe that they would be moved into real homes. After all they had been through, it seemed so fantastic that some even assumed it was all a ruse to get them out of the camp and then leave them to fend for themselves. Of the families we moved out that first day, half of them returned to the camp that evening, still unable to believe that it was all real.

The next morning, Shwan spoke with the senior men of the camp and recruited their help. I have a clear picture in my mind of him that day, standing calmly in the middle of a packed circle of suspicious, angry men, the Iraqi summer sun blasting down on us and the hot, dusty wind whirling through the compound. His patience and calm demeanor slowly settled them down. At fifty-two years old, Shwan was no child. He was a grown man whose face showed that he understood the world, and it was clear they respected him. Once he had convinced them, they moved quickly to his side. The men of the camp then spoke gently with the elderly, who were the most fearful and confused. The people gradually came to accept that this was real. Three days later, the families were all cleared out, and the following week, the camp's shelter units were hauled away, the debris plowed aside, and the surface scraped clean.

The closing down of the camp had an immediate impact throughout the entire displaced community. It showed to the people that not only was the Church paying attention to the needs of the people, but more importantly, it understood the simple need for a semblance of dignity. As Archbishop Warda would later say in an interview with members of the Nazarene Fund regarding the project, "For the first time in years, the people felt like human beings again."[2]

---

[2] Mercury One, "The Nazarene Fund – Celebrating One Year," YouTube, August 30, 2016, https://www.youtube.com/watch?time_continue=20&v=EkmQS3femTc.

Photo by Stephen M. Rasche

Fr. Shwan Kakona, Chaldean Catholic Priest of Ankawa, Erbil. A deacon with the Archdiocese of Erbil during the time of the ISIS war, he was ordained as priest in 2019. He would become one of the most trusted people in the Church to the thousands of displaced Christians and Yazidis in the camps spread throughout the city.

During the two years of its existence, the Nazarene Fund program for housing assistance would be directly responsible for the closing of five IDP camps in and around in Erbil, but it was the first that mattered most. There was no question in the minds of those of us working there that the camp had been on the verge of coming apart, and its closure brought back hope and, most importantly, time in which to hold the people together. In comparing the quick response and action made possible by the Nazarene Fund's support to the process-driven workings of the UN and USAID, it was equally clear to us that if we had waited on institutional aid, the situation would have fallen apart that summer.

* * *

IT WAS NOW MID-AUGUST 2017, and I was living then in Teleskof in the rectory with Fr. Salar. We were working daily out in the town and up the road in Batnaya, bringing visitors in and out, showing the work that was ongoing and the work that needed to be done, drafting proposals, writing reports, documenting progress, and above all else, trying to encourage the people. Every night, we were invited for dinner in the home of a different family, where we would sit late into the night talking, supporting, listening, and laughing.

The laughter of Iraqis was an incongruous thing. In a country whose history had seen decades of war and hardship, where every town, it seemed, had some form of widespread violence within living memory, the people retained a sense of humor that was always there. Wherever there were three or more Iraqis together, it seemed, within minutes, there would be laughter.

But rounding the corner and walking up the narrow road to the church in Batnaya that afternoon, nothing I saw in front of me included laughter. Three armored Chevrolet Suburbans, all fitted out with full field communications systems, were parked in front of the church entrance, along with a gathering of Kurdish security vehicles and soldiers. The Suburbans I recognized immediately as belonging to the US State Department security team from Erbil. US diplomats were regular visitors to the church facilities in Erbil. As the only American on staff, I had often been the person to walk the security teams through the compound ahead of visits and address concerns. By that time, many of the security crew members knew me by name.

"Hey Steve," a lanky, bearded American in a loose-fitting Columbia shirt waved to me.

"Hey, Mark," I returned. "Are we having visitors?"

"Ahh, guess you need to talk to the guys inside."

Coming now into the courtyard, I saw Fr. Salar standing there in a gathering of the US security team. We exchanged greetings around, and I asked what was happening.

"Well," said the team leader, "we were just sent out to check out things. You'll need to speak with the political officer back in Erbil for any more details."

I looked over to Fr. Salar, who looked at me in a confused way.

"Okay, sure enough, I'll give them a call."

I asked them if they had finished, and they said they just needed to check out a few things around the perimeter.

"There's a room in a building just around the corner filled with mostly empty mortar rounds," I said. "Russian. But a few of them are still live. We're trying to get someone out here to clear them, but we've just kept it closed off for now."

"We'll need to see that if you can show us," said the team leader.

I led two of them outside and up a narrow alleyway and gently pushed open a metal door, revealing what appeared to have once been a workshop for creating IEDs. One of the team members took some photos and made some notes. Then we headed back to join the group. After some brief small talk, they climbed into the Suburbans and drove off.

Fr. Salar looked uncomfortable.

"What is it?" I asked.

"On the phone from the consulate one hour ago, they told me only that somebody would be coming in the next days and that the security team would be here soon but that I could not say anything about to anyone."

"Okay, Padre," I said. "Don't worry. I'll call them."

I got on the phone with the local hire who worked in the political section at the consulate, our regular point of contact for low-level matters.

"Are we having a visitor?" I asked.

"Actually," he said, "I am not sure I am allowed to speak to you about it. Can you call my boss?"

His boss was the consulate political officer, a woman I was often in contact with, and I gave her a call directly. She was not in but soon emailed to ask if they could call from one of their office numbers.

When the phone rang, I picked up and was almost immediately introduced to another woman, a career State Department officer who was, apparently, in charge of the delegation that was preparing to visit.

Eventually, it came out that although the date of the visit was not certain, the planned visitors would be the US ambassador from Baghdad, Ken Silliman. He would be arriving with Brett McGurk, originally hired under the Bush administration but now a holdover from the Obama administration as special presidential envoy for the Global Coalition to Counter ISIL.[3] I told them that their visit would be a good thing, so that they could see firsthand what the situation was out in the towns, and that they could count on the Church to cooperate in the visit.

"I don't mean to sound rude," jumped in the career officer, "but you are not invited. The delegation only wants to hear from Iraqis and not any outside NGOs."

As diplomatically as possible, I answered that it was neither here nor there with me if I attended the visit. I was scheduled to fly for meetings in Europe later in the week and the uncertainty surrounding the Teleskof visit was a complication for my planning. At the same time, I was not a worker with any NGO. I was on the staff of the Catholic Church in Iraq, and one of my primary responsibilities was specifically to be there at times like this so there would be no confusion in communications, and so the Church's position could be clearly represented. Besides that, I pointed out, I was then living in the building in which they were intending to have lunch, my room not ten feet from the room in which they would all meet.

I explained all this to the career officer. She then gave a series of deflecting answers and made a comment about my being quoted in a *USA Today* article earlier in the month and my representation in Congress a year earlier as witness for the Church in support of H.R. 390. The bill, entitled the Iraq and Syria Genocide Relief and Accountability Act, sponsored by Congressman Chris Smith (R) of New Jersey and lead cosponsored by Congresswoman Anna Eshoo (D) of California, among other things, would have authorized explicit support to faith-based

---

3 Brett McGurk was then serving as the presidential envoy in the Global Coalition to Counter ISIS. In December 2018, he would resign from his position over differences with President Trump's policies.

See: Jessica Donati and Michael R. Gordon, "President Trump's Envoy in War Against Islamic State Resigns," *The Wall Street Journal*, December 22, 2018, accessed October 2019, https://www.wsj.com/articles/trumps-envoy-in-war-against-islamic-state-group-resigns-11545498028.

organizations, such as the Archdiocese of Erbil, for their humanitarian aid projects in the wake of the ISIS genocide.

"I don't know why people are even wasting their time with that bill. It violates the Establishment Clause. It's unconstitutional."[4]

Perhaps she regretted saying it, perhaps not. We had seen so many supposedly trained diplomats who were hostile to us that we were unfazed by it. But in putting it out there, she made all of her positions clear. She certainly was no friend to us.

"Look," I said, "I won't stand in the way here. I have other work to do, and plenty of it. I'll let everyone on my side know that you did not want me there, and you can have the visit you think you need."

Three days later, Fr. Salar reached out to me by phone. The visit by McGurk and Silliman had gone well, so far as he could tell. But at the same time, he was confused. McGurk had given many assurances—that the US was going to help the Christians rebuild, that they would help in the construction of schools and a hospital, and, most importantly, that they would help to remove the Kurdish security forces from the Christian towns—and he wanted to know if this was all true.

I doubted it and told Fr. Salar so. In face-to-face meetings with the NSC Director for Iraq in Washington, DC, early after the arrival of the Trump administration, I had been told that the US would not be involved in any reconstruction of destroyed buildings or new construction of needed buildings. This was firm. Help regarding structures would be limited to restoration and rehabilitation of viable existing buildings. In the year since, this had all become a standard part of the language when discussing Iraqi aid work in the US. How could McGurk now promise the US would engage in reconstruction and new construction there in Teleskof and Batnaya? How was that even within his brief?

---

4 The argument that H.R. 390, the Iraq and Syria Genocide Relief and Accountability Act, violated the Constitution stemmed from a recurring argument within a section of the government that any form of aid which went to churches, even when engaged exclusively in humanitarian efforts, was in violation of the Establishment Clause, despite a long history of US aid funding for humanitarian purposes going directly through church aid organizations. Evidently unconvinced about such arguments, H.R. 390 was a bi-partisan bill that passed both the House and Senate unanimously on December 11, 2018, a rare showing of across-the-aisle cooperation.

Finishing up in Europe, I headed to the US. And on arrival there, I reached out to our contacts at NSC, who put us in touch with a senior-level career officer at the State Department, whom I emailed the next day:

Aug 30, 2017

I write to you on the recommendation of (redacted) whom I met with yesterday. As brief background, I am a US lawyer, on staff with the Catholic Church in Northern Iraq, and among other responsibilities, specifically assigned by the Church to liaison work with the USG.

Last week a high level [sic] delegation came to Teleskov to meet with one of our Priests, Father Salar, who is the Vicar General of the Al-Qosh Diocese, and with whom I presently share residence at our rectory in Teleskov. My particular responsibility in the Al-Qosh Diocese is overall coordination of aid projects and resettlement/ stabilization. The delegation included Envoy McGurk, Ambassador Silliman, and CG Ken Gross of Erbil.

While I was not present at the meeting, Fr. Salar has shared with me the contents of the discussion as he understood them. Fr Salar understood that all three guests confirmed to him that the USG was prepared to begin working through direct funding and support with the Church, and that among the projects potentially available are those which would involve new construction (hospital, schools etc).

While we would certainly welcome such a development, this understanding is somewhat at odds with existing, in-depth discussions with the USG (AID, NSC) in which we are presently engaged. For good order's sake, I am sharing this with you so that you can verify or correct Fr Salar's [sic] understanding, and so that we can continue to coordinate our work with the USG in the most efficient manner possible.

Thank you kindly for any assistance you can provide here.

Later that same day came a response.

August 30, 2017

Steve,

Thanks for reaching out. Are you located in DC? If so, I would be happy to meet. If not, perhaps we could set up a phone call.

The United States provides a great deal of humanitarian and stabilization assistance in Iraq. The former is based on need; Iraqi Christians are equally eligible as any other group. As for stabilization, a disproportionately large part goes to minority communities. We have [sic] had tremendous success working with the UNDP's Funding Facility for Stabilization, which is a model globally for this type of work. Already 2.1 million Iraqi IDPS have returned to their homes. The US Government does not provide stabilization assistance directly to churches, or specific minority community organizations, though of course private donors do so.[5] Our Embassy in Baghdad has established a minorities working group to help link minority communities with assistance organizations.

Unable to devise an answer from the boilerplate response, I set up the call. When we finally managed to make contact, I was in the international terminal at Logan International Airport in Boston, waiting to board my next flight back to Iraq.

We exchanged pleasantries, and then I began by expressing our frustration that the clearing up of this matter had even become necessary. I went over the manner in which I had been excluded from the visit in Teleskof, reiterating that what we were speaking about now was exactly the type of harmful confusion that my presence there in Iraq was designed to avoid. I received the standard deflective answers regarding operational security and communications. He confirmed that the US would not be participating in either new construction or reconstruction of destroyed buildings. He regretted if Fr. Salar had misunderstood, and he would try to see if he could find out how that might have happened.

---

[5] The comment here that the US does not provide assistance "directly to churches" is reflective of the sentiment addressed in FN 21 above.

We then moved on to some of the claims made in his email to me, specifically his view that the UNDP efforts in Iraq were being viewed as a "tremendous success" and the basis for a "global" model. I told him that on the ground we were not seeing any of that in the Christian towns of Nineveh, and that the UNDP reports which we were seeing were completely removed from the reality of what we were experiencing. I spoke about the corruption and cosmetic nature of the contract work being performed under the UNDP and UNICEF name. I told him how Christian contractors were being kept out from the local hiring process for refusal to pay the "commission" fee to the local prime contractors, who were all non-Christians, even where the work was being done in wholly Christian towns. He listened then replied, politely, that he could not accept this information as accurate and he was not able to believe in its truth. He was a friend of Lise Grande, then the head of UNDP in Iraq, and he said if these sorts of things were going on, she would know about it and not allow it.

How could that be so, I asked, when the UN and USAID did not have their own people on the ground out there to inspect things? I explained that we knew the security teams at the UN very well, and we knew how little presence there was of the UN regular staff out in the field in the Christian towns. Why would the UN and the US not accept the good-faith input we, the Church, had to provide as to the reality of things? We had no ulterior motive. We wanted only progress for the towns so that the people could return. We wanted the UN to succeed. We did not want to replace them and, in fact, could not. But we were being faced daily with a system that was bypassing these Christian towns, while those in charge at the US and UN pointed to glossy reports which told of the progress in glowing terms. Even worse, when the US did actually show up on the site, it came in the form of murky visits such as the recent one by Brett McGurk which had the net effect of causing division, confusion, and even worse, more false hopes.

While both our demeanors were professional enough, it was clear we were speaking from vastly different realities. In his, the UN was the trusted partner of the US, and its staff was comprised of friends, all of whom were fully competent and doing good work. The stabilization effort in Iraq was a tremendous success and a model for other countries.

I told him I wished that we could see that this was true. From our view, the effort was failing, the Christians were giving up hope and leaving, and we were now very close to being out of time.

My flight was called for boarding, and we closed out the conversation politely, neither having convinced the other of anything. I walked to the other end of the terminal and back to stretch my legs before the long flight, but also to settle my mind. As I walked, a saying came into my mind back from the many years I had spent working in Mexico.

No intentes tapar el sol con un dedo. You cannot block the sun with your finger.

The truth for the Christians in Iraq would come out sooner or later, and when it did, all of the manipulation of reporting and deflection of reality would be moot. Within the year, the world would be able to see Christians successfully returned to these towns or they would not. These thoughts rolled on, how the end was coming for the Christians of Nineveh, and slowly my mind was becoming resigned to it. I stepped forward, the last in line, and boarded the Turkish Airlines flight to Istanbul.

CHAPTER 6

In the Footsteps of the Righteous

Dismayed and frustrated as we were by the numbing bureaucracy and indifference we continued to encounter with the US and the UN, not everyone had been looking away. Early on, as the violence of ISIS began to unfold, a group of voices began to speak out, isolated and small in numbers yet uniquely powerful in their moral and historical standing—the Jews.

In an opinion piece in *The Telegraph* on March 29, 2016, Rabbi Lord Jonathan Sacks wrote, "The ethnic cleansing of Christians throughout the Middle East is one of the crimes against humanity of our time, and I am appalled that there has been little serious international protest."[1]

The courage of Lord Sacks in defending the plight of the Christians in the face of this terror stood out in sharp contrast to the silence, or equivocation, of the majority of Western media and governments at the time. Seeing the persecution of the Christians as representative of a threat deserving of grave concern to all, he wrote further, "The real target is not Christianity but freedom."

---

[1] Jonathan Sacks, "We are facing an unprecedented age of terror," *The Telegraph*, March 29,2016, accessed October, 2019, https://www.telegraph.co.uk/opinion/2016/03/29/we-are-facing-an-unprecedented-age-of-terror.

Striking directly at the matter, Sacks continued, "The aim of ISIL is political: to re-establish the Caliphate and make Islam once more an imperial power. But there is another aim shared by many jihadist groups: to silence anyone and anything that threatens to express a different truth, another faith, a different approach to religious difference. That is what lay behind the attacks on the Danish cartoons; on Catholics after a speech by Pope Benedict XVI; the murder of Theo van Gogh; and the attacks on Charlie Hebdo. The calculation of the terrorists is that, in the long run, the West will prove too tired to defend its own freedoms. They are prepared to keep committing atrocities for as long as it takes, decades if need be."

Not leaving any lack of clarity as to where the change needed to be, Sacks wrote, "The world needs to hear another voice from within Islam."

Almost immediately after the depth of the ISIS wave of terror became clear, another prominent Jewish peer, Lord George Weidenfeld, stepped forward and began a private initiative to save Christians fleeing for their lives in Syria and Iraq.

In an article published in the UK edition of *The Independent* on July 14, 2015, Weidenfeld's effort was described as, "A Jewish Peer who fled occupied Austria as a child is funding the rescue of up to 2,000 Christians from Syria and Iraq as a way of showing his gratitude to the religion whose members saved him from the Nazis."[2]

Brushing aside criticism that his project was excluding Muslims, the ninety-five-year-old Weidenfeld was unapologetic. "I can't save the world, but there is a very specific possibility on the Christian side. Let others do what they like for the Muslims."

For Weidenfeld, there was a debt to pay to the Christians who had saved him and others like him in 1938. "It was a very high-minded operation and we Jews should also be thankful and do something for the endangered Christians."

The Jewish view on the importance of the Christian fiber to the world's fabric was not simply a thing brought about by pity in the face

---

2 Tom Brooks-Pollock, "Jewish peer who fled Nazis is rescuing Christians fleeing Isis to repay 'debt'," *The Independent*, July 14, 2015, accessed October, 2019, https://www.independent. co.uk/news/world/middle-east/jewish-peer-who-fled-nazis-is-rescuing-christians-fleeing-isis-to-repay-debt-10388388.html.

of ISIS murder. In a November, 2012 article in *First Things* by Matthew Schmitz titled, "Does it Make Sense to Speak of Christophobia?," Schmitz examined the 2007 writings of Jewish legal scholar J.H.H. Weiler, in his piece, *A Christian Europe: An Exploratory Essay*. Weiler wrote forcefully about the need to reject a growing dismissal of Europe's Christian roots. There, Weiler urged instead that Europe should be a place that "abandons its Christophobia and neither fears, nor is embarrassed by, the recognition that Christianity is one of the central elements in the evolution of its unique civilization."[3]

But on the ground in Iraq, this moral embrace was problematic. Inevitably in the Middle East, the Jewish story was forced into the anti-Israel narrative. Those walking in common cause with the Jews, regardless of the topic, were automatically deemed to be in league against the Arabs. As supposed co-conspirators with the Israelis, any partners would thus be considered legitimate targets by their sworn enemies, who existed seemingly everywhere in the region. For the exposed Christians in Iraq, the danger was acute. Regular rumors circulated that the missionary aid workers helping with the displaced Christians, were in fact Israeli agents and secret Jews, and that the private money funding the relief and development efforts came not from faith-based organizations in the US and Europe, but instead from the Israelis as part of a plot to infiltrate Iraq. For good order's sake, the Archdiocese of Erbil began publicly distributing quarterly reports on aid efforts in which all donors to the archdiocese were specifically identified thereby making clear the source and amounts of all donated funds. But in Iraq, the land of rumor built upon rumor with incitement always just a step away, the allegations were never completely cleared aside. Their presence sat in the background behind many later discussions with well-meaning efforts from Jewish groups around the world, in which we were forced to show ever-present caution and circumspection, fearing retribution and attacks against the people.

Ironically, at the same time the Christians were seeking to avoid any terrorist or other repercussions from any perceived alliance with Israel,

---

3 Matthew Schmitz, "Does it make sense to speak of Christophobia,"? First Things, November 29, 2012, accessed October, 2019, https://www.firstthings.com/blogs/firstthoughts /2012/11/does-it-make-sense-to-speak-of-christophobia.

it was an open secret that the Kurdistan Regional Government was continuing to develop strong relations with the Israelis, including robust cooperation in intelligence and security matters. The depth of the relationship would be proven out in the Kurdish independence referendum of 2017 when Israel stood alone among major governments in formally endorsing an independent Kurdistan.[4]

---

[4] Jeffrey Miller, "Israel endorses independent Kurdish state," *Reuters*, September 13, 2017, accessed October, 2019, https://www.reuters.com/article/us-mideast-crisis-kurds-israel/israel -endorses-independent-kurdish-state-idUSKCN1BO0QZ.

CHAPTER 7

Exam Time

It was September 2017 back in Teleskof. With the support of funds from the Hungarian government and other private donors, the town, unique amongst the other towns of Nineveh, was slowly coming back to life and the families were preparing for the return of the school year. It was late in the afternoon, and I sat in the study of the rectory with Fr. Salar and members of the reconstruction team. At the door, one of the town elders, Bassim, apologized for interrupting.

"There is a problem with the schools," he said to us. "The headmaster says they will not be ready. There has been no work done."

I looked over at Fr. Salar.

"These are the government schools," he said.

"The schools where the UN contractors have worked?" I asked, my recent conversations with the US State Department still fresh in my mind.

"Yes."

"Just the painting on the outside, yes?"

"Yes."

Bassim spoke. "The headmaster needs help from us to clean the insides of the buildings. Nothing has been done there."

"How much still needs to be done?" I asked.

"I think you should come and see," said Bassim. Fr. Salar nodded in agreement, and we headed off with Bassim, who was now on the phone with the headmaster arranging to meet us there.

The work had been done by UNICEF contractors months before, in the early days of the return to Teleskof. It had been one of the dozens of cosmetic projects we had seen so much of, and of the type I was referring to in my conversations back in the US. Designed to show positive results on professional reports that would be circulated back in New York, Washington, DC, and Brussels, the reports were often wholly disconnected from any real necessity or impact on the ground. In the Kurdish sector, these work contracts were nearly all handled by Kurdish contractors, and Christian workers were rarely employed, even in the exclusively Christian towns such as Teleskof. Reports would come to us regularly from potential Christian contractors who complained about the corruption in the contracting and implementation process. In the Iraqi-controlled sector, the UN was working through what it asserted were the proper local authorities in Telkayf, the regional municipal government center. Not surprisingly, large amounts of UNDP aid projects were being directed to the town of Telkayf itself, which the UN repeatedly listed as one of the minority Christian towns they were assisting. In reality, the Christians had all fled from Telkayf under threats and actions of violence from their Muslim neighbors, and essentially none had returned. Despite its long history of having a large Christian population, the town had, in recent decades, become a seat of radical Islamic teaching and sentiment, where ISIS sympathy ran deep. To include it on a list of "Christian" towns being provided assistance was both tragic and an insult to the Christians who had been violently forced out.

Telkayf had been retaken by Iraqi forces on January 19, 2017.[1] One week later, a Church delegation, including His Beatitude Louis Sako, Patriarch of the Chaldean Catholic Church, headed south from Teleskof to reclaim the church property there which included the Church

---

[1] Mohamed Mostafa, "Army captures Tel Kaif, Fadhilya, north of Mosul," *Iraqi News*, January 19, 2017, accessed October, 2019, https://www.iraqinews.com/iraq-war/army-recapturestel-kaif-fadhiliya-storms-mosul.

of the Sacred Heart with its ancient limestone pillars and intricately carved archways. As our convoy set out with a heavily armed Kurdish Peshmerga troop carrier escort, front and rear, the Patriarch and other notables led the line of SUVs, in which I rode with Fr. Salim and Fr. Salar.

Fr. Salar and I had been to the Kurdish front line just south of Batnaya many times during the course of the war. There we met with the Kurdish commanders, escorting important visitors, but this was our first time venturing beyond their network of entrenched observation posts and heavy gun emplacements, from which they had bombarded Telkayf and Mosul to the south. The road itself had been severed in multiple places throughout the war, and we were forced to follow a dirt track that turned and dipped across the blown-up and burned fields until we arrived at the checkpoint, where we officially crossed from the Kurdish sector and into the Iraqi-held territory. There, the escorts shifted, and we were picked up by Iraqi government security forces with only the smaller group of Christian security forces continuing forward to protect the Patriarch. After moving slowly through the rubble of shot-up and cratered buildings on the northwest perimeter, we were soon on the relatively undamaged main road into the town.

Despite the length of time it took for ISIS to be forced back from Telkayf, the main town had received little damage. The common understanding at the time was that since Telkayf had been such a loyal center of ISIS support, the fighters did not want to have heavy damage inflicted on the town and its inhabitants. Later intelligence would indicate that the ISIS fighters, squeezed from every side and running low on supplies, simply made a decision to take their stand in Mosul and retreated there without wasting further men and ammunition in Telkayf.

As our column roared up the main road, the platoon of Iraqi security forces sat with their weapons at the ready, staring down fiercely from their truck platforms at the townspeople walking by on the roadside. Young boys, having had their town overrun before and understanding the game even at their early age, ran alongside, waving the "V" sign, while women in full black Niqab dress moved quickly behind them, looking straight ahead or glancing only for a second at the passengers in our cars.[2] Inside our caravan, the cars all had rosaries hung from the rear-view mirrors, and the cars themselves were filled with priests, sisters, and other Christian leaders. Standing further back from the road were groups of men, all clean-shaven, staring at us unflinchingly, without emotion.

"Two weeks ago," said Fr. Salim, "they all would have killed us."

As the column turned off the main road and wound its way through a series of narrow streets to the back entrance of the church, we felt, for the first time, vulnerable. The column came to a stop, and the Iraqi soldiers all jumped down, spreading out to form a rough perimeter, while the Christian security forces surrounded the Patriarch and cleared the way for him to enter the church courtyard. There, jumping in front of the crowd to be the first to welcome, and dropping to his knees, came a thick and grizzled man from the nominally Christian-led militia, the "Babylon Brigade." He was shouting greetings at the Patriarch, who motioned him to get up and moved quickly past. Just days later, the same man's photo would be posted on local social media with a wide malevolent smile, his foot standing on the throat of an alleged ISIS supporter. US military liaison officers in Erbil would eventually identify him as a former criminal who had been arrested for murder during the US occupation.

Inside the church, the sanctuary had been swept out and the entire space was bare, save for a simple wooden lectern standing where the altar had once been. Apart from the hundreds of bullet scars where every Christian symbol had been shot off, the church was almost clean. Coming midway into the sanctuary, the Patriarch stood ringed by other clergy and officials, who sang out some traditional prayers. Then the Patriarch gave a short speech after which a group of men climbed up onto the roof of the church, and placed a new cross up on the dome. From the church, looking across to the Christian cemetery on the hill nearby, the gravestones had all been knocked down and smashed, the

---

2 The "V" sign originated with Winston Churchill as "V for Victory" in WWII. Since then it has become a global sign seen often in times of strife. See: Nathaniel Zelinsky, "From Churchill to Libya: How the V symbol went viral," *Washington Post*, March 25, 2011, accessed October 2019, https://www.washingtonpost.com/opinions/from-churchill-to-libya-how-the-v-symbol -went-viral/2011/03/18/AFzPiYYB_story.html.

stone slab tombs heaved open and desecrated. The bell, restored by then back into the bell tower, was rung out—its sound cutting clearly across the town for the first time in two and half years—amidst a somehow mournful jubilation from the small crowd. And then we all climbed back down the stairs, settled back into our cars and trucks, and drove away, out of the Iraqi sector, back into no-man's land, past the bomb craters and carcasses of dead animals, back into the Kurdish sector, and on up the road. For most of us who made the visit that day, we would not make any plans to return.

Months later, when UNDP reports touted the funds spent on the restoration of the Christian town of Telkayf, the Church pushed back. When complaints about the misleading nature of the UN reports were laid before those in the aid pipeline in Washington, DC, the response was always that any such complaints must be mistaken and based on bad information. But we were living amidst the work product of these contracts and in the reality of these towns. We saw the truth of what was being done. Someday this truth would come out.

Meanwhile, in Teleskof, we knew that while the schools might have been a glaring example of this misleading, even corrupt, behavior, still they needed to be opened soon, so we would see what could be done to help.

After a short walk, Bassim and I met the headmaster at the gate of the first school on the tour, the public school for boys. Prominently stenciled in fresh blue paint just to the right of the gate was the UNICEF name and logo. All the exterior vertical spaces on the cement walls surrounding the compound had been freshly painted as well. But the twelve-inch thick walls had not received any paint on either the top or the interior. The work had been cynically done for photo purposes only, to show it as complete from the street or a distance, a contractor's trick we had seen many times. Thinking that we might, at some point, reach somebody who would actually listen, I took out my iPhone and began taking pictures to document it all. These were schools after all, and the UNICEF logo was everywhere.

We stepped inside and looked about at the burned-out, blackened yard space, trash heaped up in the corners, scorched remains of large bushes blown across a cracked and heaved walkway to the main building

Photo by Stephen M. Rasche

Public School in Teleskof, Nineveh Plain, Northern Iraq, just after UNICEF contractors had "completed" restoration of the school in September, 2017. The
restoration consisted of one thin coat of paint on the exterior walls and the stenciled spray painting of the UNICEF logo.

entrance. Reaching the front door, the outside walls again were all
freshly painted, with a large blue UNICEF logo newly stenciled just next
to the entryway. But once inside, it was clear, once again, that nothing
else had been done.

In the classrooms, what furniture remained was covered in dust
and broken, pushed up into piles against the back walls of the rooms.
Ceilings and walls were lined with deep cracks and plaster falling down
in slabs onto dust and trash-covered floors. In room after room, it was
the same situation. When we came outside, the headmaster brought us
down to the water main and showed us the broken main valves, unre-
paired. As for electricity, there was hope that the schoolmaster might
soon be able to splice a new line in from a nearby private generator, but

Photo by Stephen M. Rasche

Interior of the school in Teleskof showing "completed" work of UNICEF contractors.

the UNICEF contracting work itself had not touched any of the electrical system inside the school.

The headmaster then took us a short distance away to the school for girls, where the tour was a repeat finding of the conditions from the other school buildings and grounds.

Out back on the sidewalk now, finished with the pictures, we talked. If the people would help, enough rooms could be cleared and cleaned to open the schools on time, in two weeks. The electricity was not so critical; the window shutters could be opened, and there would be plenty of light. The headmaster was concerned about the water, though. Something needed to be done. He could not open without water.

As we walked back to the church, Bassim spoke.

"This work, this is not right. Your government, they cannot do anything about this?" he asked me.

"They say that this responsibility belongs to the UN, and the UN is their trusted partner. Really, when we try to tell them these things, they do not want to hear it from us."

We walked on a bit further, the sun now going low and the shadows beginning to provide some cover along the sidewalk.

"I will send these pictures back to our friends in the US anyhow," I said. "I will speak again there soon. We will see."

* * *

By October 3, 2017, I was back in Washington, DC, seated in a hearing room at the Rayburn Office Building. I testified as a witness on behalf of the Church before the House Foreign Affairs Committee regarding the status of the return of Christians to the Nineveh Plain and, in particular, the status surrounding US and UN aid policy and implementation. Testifying alongside me, among others, was former Congressman Frank Wolf, (R) of Virginia, a long-time fighter for oppressed minorities around the world who had recently come back from a fact-finding mission in northern Iraq, during which we had met and conferred several times. I had testified similarly a year earlier in September of 2016, at that time simply trying to bring attention to the urgency of the issue, the work we were trying to do, who was funding it and who, including the US and the UN, was not. Returning again to provide an update, among the supplemental evidence I had submitted as part of my testimony, were the pictures of the schools from Teleskof which I had managed to enter into the record just ahead of the deadline. Addressing my remarks to the chairman, Congressman Chris Smith (R) of New Jersey, excerpts of the testimony from myself and Congressman Wolf went as follows:[3]

---

[3] US House of Representatives, Committee on Foreign Affairs, *Iraq and Syria Genocide Emergency Relief and Accountability*, October 3, 2017. Accessed October 2019. https://foreignaffairs.house.gov/2017/10/iraq-and-syria-genocide-emergency-relief-and-accountability.

Mr. SMITH. I would now ask that Mr. Rasche begin his testimony. I would point out that when Mr. Rasche testified almost a year ago to the day, September 22nd, before us he said, "It is no exaggeration to say without these private donors"—and he pointed out the Knights of Columbus, Aid to the Church in Need, Caritas of Italy, had provided some $26 million at that point—"the situation for Christians in northern Iraq would have collapsed and the vast majority of these families would, without question, have already joined the refugee diaspora now destabilizing the Middle East and Europe."

He pointed out that throughout the entirety of the crisis since August 2014, other than an initial supply of tents and tarps, the Christian community in Iraq has received nothing in aid from the U.S. aid agencies or the United Nations. Which I found appalling at the time which is why, again, this is the 10th hearing in a series that we have had. We had administration witnesses appear. We pleaded with them to provide that aid. They always say they would look into it. And then nothing happened.

But, again, I look forward to your testimony now, especially in light of you having lived this. You have been the IDP person. It must be agonizing to know that the resources should be there and have not been.

STATEMENT OF MR. STEPHEN RASCHE, LEGAL COUNSEL, DIRECTOR OF INTERNATIONALLY DISPLACED PERSONS ASSISTANCE, CHALDEAN CATHOLIC ARCHDIOCESE OF ERBIL

Mr. RASCHE. Thank you, Mr. Chairman, for giving me the opportunity to come back and speak to you again.

Again, my name is Stephen Rasche. And I come to you from Erbil in northern Iraq, but most recently ... from the towns of Batnaya and Teleskov ...where I spend most of my time these days, along with the other Christian towns out in the Iraqi sector.

In my work in Erbil I serve on the staff of the Catholic Archdiocese of Erbil. And in that context I serve as legal counsel for external affairs, the Director of IDP Resettlement Programs, which includes the Nineveh Reconstruction Project.

Since 2014, the Archdiocese of Erbil has provided almost all the medical care, food, shelter, and education for the more than 100,000 Christians that fled ISIS, as well as many Yazidis and Muslims who are also in our care. Mr. Chairman, I wish I could tell you that in the 12 months that followed since my last appearance here that our pleas have been heard and that our plight had found relief. But as I speak before you now, I regret to say that we have still yet to receive any form of meaningful aid from the U.S. Government.

While we have found the political appointees much more willing to help us since January, the fact is that even after the better part of a year they have been unable to move the bureaucracy to take meaningful action. Last month, Secretary of State Rex Tillerson reaffirmed that Iraq's religious minorities were the victims of genocide. But even that declaration, combined with the statutory mandate—statutory mandate to aid these communities with funds allocated for fiscal year 2017 by Congress in the Consolidated Appropriations Act for May, has been insufficient to create action on the part of these agencies.

The fiscal year ended days ago, with these agencies continuing to shirk their statutory obligations. Still no aid has been provided to the imperiled Christian minority.

These humanitarian principles are intended to prevent aid from being used to punish or reward religious, national, or racial groups. It was and is incomprehensible to us that these principles have been interpreted and applied to prohibit intentionally helping religious and ethnic minority communities to survive genocide. Interestingly, these principles were waived last month when the Department of State's Bureau for Population, Refugees, and Migration provided 32 million in emergency humanitarian assistance to the Rohingya Muslims, a religious minority in Burma.

As an American, I am proud when my country responds to a humanitarian crisis, but this action begs the question of why the State Department, which has distributed over $220 million in humanitarian assistance in Iraq since 2014, has consistently ignored the dire needs of the persecuted minorities in Iraq.

Given this, H.R. 390, the Genocide Relief Act, is a vital lifeline we have desperately needed for months. The House of Representatives passed it unanimously on June the 6th, and the Senate Foreign Relations Committee passed it unanimously on September 19th, yet still it sits in the Senate. We hope that they will consider our existential plight, and that time is short for us, and make it law soon.

Mr. Chairman, had we received any kind of proper assistance from the U.S. Government for the nearly 100,000 displaced Christians in our care who had to flee ISIS, we would by now have been able to resettle the vast majority of them back into their homes in the recovered towns of Nineveh. Instead, our pool of private donors and already limited funds have dwindled. We had hoped to use these resources for the return of displaced Christians. Instead, we had to repurpose much of these funds for the ongoing humanitarian needs of these same displaced people.

We are, thus, faced with the excruciating decision of whether to continue keeping our people housed and fed in temporary shelters in Erbil, or return them to their destroyed towns with only the barest funds to rebuild in Nineveh.

To close up here I would say to you we are now caught in a situation where we are fully exposed and at risk, and finding ourselves at a critical, historical inflection point. While status reports from the UNDP work in Nineveh purport to show real progress in the Christian majority towns, on the ground we see little evidence of it. Work projects are in most cases cosmetic in nature, and much of that cynically so. Completed school rehabilitation projects in Teleskov, and Batnaya, and Bartella take the form of one thin coat of painting on the exterior surface walls, with freshly stenciled UNICEF logos every 30 feet. Meanwhile, inside the rooms remain untouched and unusable. There is no water. There is no power. There is no furniture.

I have pictures that I can show you of these worksites later on in the question and answer period that give a pretty clear picture of what the nature of the work is there.

One more thing that I would like to note is in the UNDP reports claiming to show the work being done in areas in which religious minorities are the majority, prominently list work in the formerly

Christian town of Telkayf. A copy of this report has been distributed to this committee. Mr. Chairman, there are no more Christians in Telkayf. They were forced from this town by acts of genocide, crimes against humanity, and war crimes. ISIS was firmly in control of this town until last fall, and many of its Sunni Arab residents remain. Many of those residents who openly welcomed ISIS while simultaneously engaging in forced and violent expulsion of the Christian majority are still there.

Telkayf has also been chosen as a settlement site for the families of slain ISIS fighters. As such, 100 percent of the work being done in this town benefits the Sunni Arab residents of the town, and there is no consideration anywhere in U.N. aid planning for the displaced Christians, who now depend wholly upon the church and private sources for their survival.

In testimony from former Congressman Wolf, similar points were made.

After a week visiting Bartella, Qaraqosh, Duhok, Erbil, Mosul, Nimrud, Mt. Sinjar, and Sinjar City in August and talking with individuals in the various communities, I am sad to say that if bold action is not taken by the end of the year, I believe a tipping point will be reached and we will see the end of Christianity in Iraq in a few short years and a loss of religious and ethnic diversity throughout the region, a loss which will not be regained and could result in further destabilization and violent extremism and terrorism across the Middle East. In other word, ISIS will have been victorious in their genocidal rampage unless concrete action is taken.

Iraq is a land rich with Biblical history. Abraham was born there, Daniel lived and died there, and many events in the Bible took place in Iraq. And yet, we have already seen the Christian population drop from 1.5 million to 250,000, or less, over the course of the last 14 years. This exodus continues with additional families leaving every day in search of physical security, economic security, and education.

Having spent the past 3 years as Internally Displaced People, IDPs, many Christian families are at a crossroads, having to decide whether or not they should return to their newly liberated villages or leave Iraq forever. Despite their best efforts, many believe that they can stay only if bold action is taken by the United States Government and other international partners to ensure, ensure their future security.

Unfortunately, to a large extent, U.S. Government assistance has not been forthcoming to Iraq's Christians and Yazidi communities even though the President, the Vice President, Congress, and Secretary of State have declared them victims of genocide. Many of the displaced Christians, for example, have had to seek the mainstay of their aid from private charitable sources on a piecemeal basis over the last 3 years. This is becoming more difficult, Mr. Chairman, as many individuals who give to humanitarian organizations are facing donor fatigue.

Since 2014, Congress has had well over 40 different hearings related to ISIS, including at least seven specifically on the topic of the religious minorities, and required the State Department, the U.S. Agency for International Development to spend some funds on assistance specifically for genocide survivors from religious and ethnic minorities. Congressional resolve, and the force of law, must be matched by administration action.

Wolf then went on to outline several proposed critical action items as follows:

A Presidential Decision Directive or Presidential memorandum should be issued directing the State Department and USAID to immediately, to immediately address the needs to communities identified by Secretary Tillerson as having been targeted for genocide. This would address both humanitarian aid for those living as IDPs and refugees, and stabilization assistance for those returning to the areas.

And further:

Congress should immediately pass H.R. 390, the bipartisan Iraq and Syria Genocide Emergency Relief and Account- ability Act, authored by you and co-authored by Congresswoman Anna Eshoo. It gives explicit authorization for the State Department and USAID to identify the assistance needs of genocide survivors from religious and ethnic minority communities and provide funding to entities, including faith-based entities, effectively providing them with aid on the ground.

It is essential because some within the State Department and USAID have claimed they lack the authority to deliberately help religious and ethnic communities, even if they are genocide victims. They are genocide victims. They may be Christians, they may be Yazidis. They are genocide victims and they will become extinct, extinct without assistance.

Although there is nothing in U.S. law preventing them from helping genocide-surviving communities, the authorization will help ensure that aid actually flows to the victims. The House passed the bill, Senate Foreign Relations passed it on September 19th. The Senate should pass it quickly so it can be sent back to the House and for the President to sign it.

Mr. Chairman, in closing, there is still time but the hour is late. And we are about to run out of time. We cannot—history will judge the administration, the Congress, and the West—allow ISIS to be successful in their genocide.

In the questions that followed Congresswoman Tulsi Gabbard, (D) Hawaii, an Iraq war veteran, raised the issue of aid assistance and accuracy of reporting.

Ms. GABBARD. Lastly, Mr. Rasche, you know we have heard a number of times over the last several months from different officials within the State Department about this $100 million in assistance that they claim has been disbursed in Iraq for the religious and ethnic minority groups, including the Yazidis, Christians, and Shia. However, this number has never been quantified for us about how it has been delivered, how it has been delivered, what kind of impact it has made. And they have not provided an explanation about why this number dates all the way back to 2008.

With a year on the ground you have got a close pulse on what is happening there. If you can provide any real view on this statement that the State Department continues to make?

Mr. RASCHE. Well, I think the—you mentioned, rightly so, that they had to stretch back to 2008 in order to get that number which I think is indicative of how far the reaches have to go in order to make it appear that things are really happening.

I can simply say that on the ground we don't see it. And we tell people this. And when we tell them, we don't see this, we don't see this money that you say is being spent here, the response is generally, "Well, it is being sent, it is being spent. We have a report that says so." This is the common response that we get. And this puts us in a difficult position because, sure, we don't want to spend our time bashing the U.N. We would like to be singing their praises. But at the same time, we are responsible for taking care of these people. And we see this work, it is objectively not happening the way it is being described.

And I have just come back from a similar visit to the U.K. where we spoke with the DFID minister, their equivalent of the USAID. And they are having the same issue there trying to match the granularity of reports with what people are actually seeing on the ground.

And so it is a common problem. I don't think it is just unique here to the U.S. And it has to do with the fact that the verification of this work is being left to the people who do the work. And that is not a system that you accept anywhere. And why we accept it in a situation where we are spending hundreds of millions of dollars and where people's lives are fundamentally at risk based upon the outcomes, it is, this is the heart of it.

And as Congressman Wolf pointed out in his trip over there, you can't miss the disconnect that is going on between the reporting and what is actually happening on the ground. And the solution for that is better reporting by your own people. You cannot let the people doing the work report on what a great job they are doing because they are doing a great job always.

CHAPTER 8

Promises

The two months that followed were a whirlwind. From the US, I flew to Rome for a two-day conference on the return of Christians to Nineveh sponsored by Aid to the Church in Need International. From there, it was on to Manchester, England, where I met up with Fr. Salar and the tireless workers of Aid to the Church in Need UK, and we headed off on a tour of England to raise awareness for the plight of persecuted Christians around the globe. Included in our delegation was his Grace, Bishop Matthew Kukah of the Diocese of Sokoto in Northern Nigeria, deep in the lands then being terrorized by Boko Haram. Together we traveled the length of England by rail and car, telling our stories to school assemblies, college groups, and adult lecture forums. Manchester, Liverpool, Winchester, Lancaster, Cambridge, and London. On a rainy, windswept morning in Lancaster, I walked up the hillside park, up above the Cathedral of St. Peter, to the modest stone memorial set as a marker for the dozens of Catholics, many of them priests, who had been hung, drawn, and quartered in various places throughout the town during the English reformation just over 400 years ago. Standing in the rain for some time, we prayed for them all.

In Liverpool, Fr. Salar and I walked the length of Hope Street between the Catholic Cathedral of Christ the King and the immense

Anglican Cathedral Church of Christ. Walking up St. James's Mount to the Gothic revival masterpiece, we stepped inside, immediately in awe of the massive space above and around us, the strength and power of its architecture at first almost overwhelming. After a time wandering around, listening to the choir then in practice, we came back outside and stopped, looking back over the city. We had been in England then for over a week.

"Tell me, Stephen," said Fr. Salar. "Look at this." He waved his arm across the panorama in front of us. "Beautiful. And these people live in this beautiful country. But our people must live where the rest of the people want to kill us. Why? I want to know this."

He was silent for a time, and I had no answer.

"This money," he continued, "this money we are helping to raise, with this money we could take our whole town out of Iraq and to some-place safe, no? And who are we to tell them to stay? For what? Why should they not live in peace in a beautiful country like this?"

Throughout the entire trip to England, the situation in Iraq had been rapidly falling apart as Iraqi forces began to move north into the Kurdish-controlled regions in the aftermath of the Kurdish independence referendum. Fr. Salar's people in Teleskof were afraid, and he spent more and more time on the phone getting frantic updates as the days went by.

"Maybe, Padre," I said, "it will come to this. For now, all we can do is try until it is clear that there is nothing left to try for. This is our role, and only God knows why we are in it. Maybe soon our role will be to get the people out. Maybe very soon. But I think we will know when this time comes."

He fixed his jaw and shook his head. He was anxious for his people and for everything in front of them now. A few hours later, back outside the Catholic Cathedral of Christ the King, we gave a joint interview to a collection of UK journalists, urging the international community to pay attention to the situation unfolding then in northern Iraq, warning that if major fighting broke out, it would mean the end of the Christians still there. Two days later, Fr. Salar would be home with them, and their story would continue.

Meanwhile, I flew off to Budapest for follow-up meetings from a conference on Christians in the Middle East where an exhibit had opened using artifacts from the recovered Christian towns of Nineveh. I had been the guide in Iraq for the Hungarian team that had collected the artifacts and had been asked to make a short presentation on the status of reconstruction in Teleskof, for which the Hungarian government had been the primary donor.

There, at the airport in Budapest, on October 26, 2017, I was on my way to Rome for a conference at the Pontifical Gregorian University before returning to Iraq. It was then I first began to receive reports of the speech Vice President Pence gave, where he had announced that the US would make a policy shift and begin moving away from ineffective UN programs and instead would direct the State Department to begin sending US aid funding directly through USAID to faith-based partners and other NGOs with a proven track record on the ground.

Speaking to a supportive audience at the JW Marriott in Washington, DC, the vice president laid out the new policy and the basis supporting it.[1]

"Here's the sad reality," he began, speaking of the UN reporting on Nineveh, "The United Nations claims that more than 160 projects are in Christian areas, but for a third of those projects, there are no Christians to help."

"Projects that are supposedly marked "finished" have little more than a UN Flag hung outside an unusable building, in many cases a school.

"And while faith-based groups with proven track records and deep roots in these communities are more than willing to assist, the United Nations too often denies their funding requests. My friends, those days are over.

"Our fellow Christians and all who are persecuted in the Middle East should not have to rely on multinational institutions when America can help them directly. And tonight, it is my privilege to announce that President Trump has ordered the State Department to stop funding ineffective relief efforts at the United Nations. And from this day

---

[1] "Remarks by the Vice President at In Defense of Christians Solidarity Dinner," October 25, 2017, accessed October, 2019, https://www.whitehouse.gov/briefings-statements/remarks-vice-president-defense-christians-solidarity-dinner.

forward, America will provide support directly to persecuted communities through USAID.

"We will no longer rely on the United Nations alone to assist persecuted Christians and minorities in the wake of genocide and the atrocities of terrorist groups. The United States will work hand-in-hand from this day forward with faith-based groups and private organizations to help those who are persecuted for their faith.

"This is the moment. Now is the time. And America will support these people in their hour of need."

What this "support" would be was left undefined, but we had no doubt that "these people" included the displaced Christians of Iraq. Sitting there in the airport in Budapest, reading all the congratulatory emails flying back and forth, I drank my coffee with growing unease. How many people would now come out of the woodwork looking for a place in this new funding paradigm? Were we now just seeing the fight shift from one battle to another? As grateful as we were for the public support, we needed help, not speeches.

Meanwhile in Iraq, tensions between the Iraqi federal government and the Kurdistan regional government continued to deteriorate. Back in Teleskof, Fr. Salar was in a desperate situation in the middle of the standoff between Iraqi and Kurdish units. In Erbil, the airport had been shut down to all international commercial air traffic, meaning my return would have to be routed through Baghdad. In Washington, DC, the wiser members of the loose coalition who had been fighting in support of the Mideast Christians awaited the details of the new policy which had been outlined by Vice President Pence.

The first move out of the starting block was not encouraging. Seeking to show immediate action but perhaps unsure as to how to move about such a large bureaucratic ship so quickly, the USAID machinery posted a "Broad Agency Announcement (BAA)" that invited humanitarian NGOs to submit "concept" papers to the agency's Peer and Scientific Review Board by November 30, 2017. Following, the selected concept proposals would move to a "co-creation" phase in January of 2018, for eventual decisions on funding later that spring. There was no indication in the announcement that any UN funding was being repurposed.

Response from informed media in the US demonstrated that they were not impressed. In a lengthy article on November 1, 2017, by the then editor-at-large at Fox News, George Russell, he wrote of the USAID announcement, "The long string of exploratory stages hardly underscored the idea of emergency action."[2]

The next night, on a nationally-broadcast Fox News Insider report, host Laura Ingraham directly asked the question, "Is the Deep State resisting the White House Plan to Aid Christians and other minorities in the Middle East?"[3] Her interview panel included Nina Shea of the Hudson Institute, a tireless and courageous advocate for the persecuted Christians and minorities of the Middle East, who spoke of the failures within the UN system to address the issues facing the Christians and Yazidis in Iraq. While Shea spoke pointedly about the UNICEF-funded school projects in Teleskof, the background rolled with the photos I had shot on my iPhone with Bassim weeks earlier.

Behind the scenes, the experienced political insiders who supported the vice president's general announcement were growing equally alarmed at another issue. The speech of the vice president in itself was fine, but where was the all-important executive order? Without the formal backing of such an order, those further down in the management chain of USAID and the State Department would be left without clear instruction on any new direction and purpose of policy. From a more partisan viewpoint, without an explicit executive order or other presidential directive, those career and holdover officials who opposed the policy outlined by the vice president would be given cover to continue business as usual and attempt to run out the clock until a hoped-for change in administration in 2020.

For reasons as yet unclear, no written executive order or presidential directive was ever issued. In the ensuing years, sympathetic career staff at the State Department and USAID would consistently point to the

---

2 George Russell, "Amid Pence promises, persecuted Iraqi Christians still in perilous limbo," Fox News, November 1, 2017, accessed October, 2019, https://www.foxnews.com/world /amid-pence-promises-persecuted-iraqi-christians-still-in-perilous-limbo.

3 Laura Ingraham, "Is the 'Deep State' Resisting WH Plan to Aid Christians & Other Minorities in the Middle East?", Fox News, The Ingraham Angle, Nov. 3, 2017, accessed October, 2019, https://insider.foxnews.com/2017/11/03/ingraham-angle-pulls-back-curtain -resistance-trump-plan-aid-refugees-middle-east.

lack of any written directive as a built-in roadblock to the changes outlined by the vice president's speech. Within the Church, we were simply bewildered by it all, still in desperate need of immediate help and unable to see clearly where any of this would lead. We had been through the struggle of the genocide designation and seen nothing of any substance come from it, and we remained wary that, in this new episode, we were simply looking at a different chapter of the same story.

In Rome, I finished up the conference at the Gregorian and flew to Istanbul and, a day later, arrived in the dust, chaos, and menace that was Baghdad.

* * *

WHEN FIRST OPENED IN 1982, Saddam International Airport, as it was then known, was among the most modern airports in the Middle East. From there, it had seemingly been a never-ending downward slide through thirty-five years of disrepair and neglect, brought on by war, embargo, and more war. But the Iraqi immigration officers, eager now to be friends with Americans in the aftermath of the Kurdish Referendum in which the US had, for all outward appearances, sided with Baghdad, looked approvingly at my US passport, welcoming me in friendly English.

There had been no choice then but to fly through Baghdad, as the airport in Erbil had been firmly closed to all international traffic by the Iraqi government. There had been no statement at all as to when, or if, the Iraqis would authorize its re-opening. All indications at the time were that the central government in Baghdad was intent now on punishing the Kurds by strangling them economically, at least for a time. The route to northern Iraq, for the foreseeable future, was now through Baghdad. In Rome, I had discussed the matter with His Beatitude Patriarch Sako, who was visiting there as well. The Patriarch had insisted to me that my work in Iraq should continue, and I was provided with rooms in the rectory in Baghdad with His Beatitude and Bishop Basilio.

For me personally, I welcomed the change, as it might, I hoped, allow us to open another front in our efforts to preserve the Christian fabric of Iraq. While the focus of the Christian aid organizations had been on Nineveh and the north since the ISIS invasion of 2014, the plight of the

Christians in the south remained. While diminished greatly in numbers, many Christian parishes survived, serving people with deep faith and who were intent on remaining, and providing a continuing Christian witness to the war-ravaged city that had, for more than a millennium and a half, been their home. But they needed help, in some ways even more than in the north. In the internal diaspora from the ISIS war, not all Christians had fled to Erbil. Thousands had instead ended up in Baghdad, and no help had been directed their way.

By late 2017, the gruesome civil strife of everyday Baghdad had begun to recede. Such terror-driven violence that occurred was almost entirely driven by the Sunni-Shia divide. The Christians, beaten down into such a small number, seemed largely off the radar for attacks, perhaps no longer seen as an entity worthy of being acknowledged as any kind of threat. Another view, prominent amongst the Christians themselves, was that the Iraqis had realized that if the Christians disappeared completely, the West would be given one more reason to simply abandon the fate of the city. In the bottomless swamp of deception and connivance that formed the psyche of Baghdad, this was certainly not an unreasonable assessment.

And yet some signs pointed to something different, perhaps more elemental. While the Christians are, under both Shar'ia law and, effectively, the Iraqi constitution, citizens of a lower class, that did not mean that all elements of Christianity were without respect amongst the entirety of the Muslim population. In Baghdad and in much of Shia Iraq, this is especially so in the veneration of Mary, the Mother of Christ. Nowhere is this shown more clearly than at the Chaldean Church of the Virgin Mary in Baghdad.

There, young and middle-aged Shia women, all in black Hijab, gather regularly outside the church entrance in the courtyard at the statue of the Virgin Mary, lighting votive candles and making their silent prayers concerning the trials and hopes of motherhood. This is not to say that Islam and the Qur'an lack their own independent approach to the veneration of Mary. In fact, Mary is the only woman mentioned by name in the Qur'an, and her treatment there as the virgin mother of Jesus, is, if anything, more extensive than in the New Testament. And yet, in the manner of the specific veneration of the Apostolic Christian churches

98

Photo by Stephen M. Rasche

Muslim women light candles in the courtyard shrine at the Chaldean Catholic Church of the Virgin Mary Queen of the Rosary in Baghdad, Winter 2017.

for Mary, a natural attraction clearly exists for many Muslim women who are outwardly devout to their own faith in every other way.

"They are here every day," said Fr. Martin, speaking to me after the evening Mass. "They love Mary and look for her help."

Martin had still been a transitional deacon in the St. Peter's Seminary in Erbil when I first met him in 2015. He was from Karemlesh and had known Fr. Thabet from childhood. His family home had been destroyed, just as Thabet's, in the ISIS war and now the rest of his family had emigrated and were living in the thriving Chaldean community in San Diego, California. He had been offered a place in the safety of the Church in San Diego, but Martin was determined to stay with his people in Iraq, where, alongside Fr. Thabet, they held the displaced people of Karemlesh together during the displacement, serving their needs at the complex of rented buildings and caravans that had become their temporary village in Erbil. When he was ordained as a priest in September of 2016, he was sent for additional formation in Baghdad before being given the Parish of Mary the Virgin, where he was, as always, all energy and smiles.

The vulnerable state of the churches that spread throughout Baghdad was undeniable. Surrounding all the churches, security teams blocked off the entrances to the streets, and barbed wire ringed the high blast walls protecting the church compounds. In the Shia areas, which had overrun many of the once Christian neighborhoods, the flag of Hussein, the Shia martyr, flew everywhere, surrounding the Christian churches now isolated in their shadows. Visiting with one church after another, I took notes and tried to assess their needs and sat in their Masses, counting the numbers of parishioners, wondering, in truth, what future for them there might be. And then it was on to Basra.

Once a city of elegance, canals, culture, and wealth, the cosmopolitan port of Basra had graced the shore of the Shatt-al-Arab. It was the confluence of the Tigris and the Euphrates, just above the entrance to the Persian Gulf. In the romantic tales of Sinbad the Sailor, his ship set sail from Basra. Agatha Christie, along with thousands of British and Western expatriates, visited and lived in Basra up until the 1950s. But that city, a mix of the wealth and domineering power of the West and the ancient voice and history of the East, has long since been destroyed.

Basra in 2017 was a sprawling dump of nearly three million people, many of them living in abject poverty that was among the worst on earth. It was the site of heavy fighting and sustained shelling during the Iran-Iraq war, then home to major civil unrest against Saddam Hussein in 1991. Basra was already a heavily damaged and reeling city when the US invasion began in 2003. In the following years, the city became the scene of some of the heaviest fighting in the war, as first the British army sought to bring the city under control. Later the Iraqi army itself entered into heavy conflict with the Mahdi army and other militias. By 2017, Basra was a barely functioning nightmare of competing militias and corrupt power factions, surrounded by a swarming mass of unemployed and displaced refugees from the last two decades of conflict throughout the south of Iraq.

In the midst of this remained fewer than 300 Christian families, down from thousands at the end of the prior century. In a city which once held over a dozen Chaldean parishes, only one remained fully open by 2017. There, in the Cathedral of Our Lady, Archbishop Habib Al-Naufali, struggled on to find purpose and survival for what was now barely even a remnant church. His was now, he said, a missionary church.

Drawing strength from the example of the Saint Mother Theresa of Calcutta, the small staff of the church in Basra saw their mission as to serve and, in their service, to provide a Christian witness to the entire city. Nowhere was this more prominently demonstrated than in the elementary school run by two aging Dominican Sisters. In a school of several hundred students, less than one percent were Christian; the others were all Muslim.

Meanwhile, the once-thriving churches were nearly all shut down and boarded up. While the Church still held ownership in principle, on the grounds of many of the churches Muslim squatters had taken over. They surrounded the churches with market stalls and makeshift homes, such that the archbishop and his priests had to seek permission to gain access to the churches to check on their condition, on the rare occasions when they were able to go. In the courtyards and buildings of several unused churches, displaced Christian families had been given refuge, but the Diocese had no money to provide proper care and the conditions for the families were very poor. Driving throughout the city with Archbishop Habib, I could not help but think that this might be the future for the remains of Christianity in Iraq.

After returning to Baghdad, I set about making inquiries from among our private donor bases and government sources as well for help in Basra. The answers were nearly uniform—our donors, or our directives, have provided us with funds for Nineveh, and that is our priority for now. For Archbishop Habib and the Christians of Basra, they would have to wait. In the months to come, I would think of them often, living patiently in their poverty, doing their best to provide a Christian witness of service in the midst of overwhelming antagonism and marginalization. It shamed me deeply that, in leaving their needs aside, all of us were missing something that ought to have struck at the core of who we should have been. The decades of war and persecution had flung the remaining Christians throughout Iraq, and now we were turning away from the least of them simply because they were so small in number.

I could not then, and cannot now, square it with any of the Christian teachings which we professed to believe.

While I stayed with the Patriarch and Bishop Basilio, the UN mission learned of my presence there and sent over an emissary, a senior manager from UNICEF who came to the rectory one day and sat with myself and the Patriarch to offer up an apology for what had taken place with the schools in Teleskof. They had been moving too quickly for their own good, he said, and had lost track of some the work that was being done. We thanked him for his time and the apology but explained that it was not our view that this was an isolated case, urging him for closer attention to the situation. Apparently chastened, he left the rectory, and I never heard from him again.

But all this was shallow progress. Our goal was not to be muckrakers against the UN and the US aid system, as beneficial to taxpayers, aid donors and recipients as that may have been. Our goal was to save a people, and in that, this constant battling with the US and the UN was becoming an increasingly overwhelming distraction rather than a solution. We did not have the people or the funds to keep this up, and our time was running out. Privately, I had been telling people we had until the end of summer 2017 to move a critical mass of people back into the towns so as to prevent their being taken over by other circling power factions. Here we were now, heading into the winter of 2018, and for many of us, we had the growing sense that our time was all but done.

CHAPTER 9

In the Diaspora

Noor sat across the table from me. It was April of 2018, and I had known him for nearly two years by then, enough to know he was deeply distressed.

"I cannot stay any longer," he said. "I will leave this month."

Noor was a Syriac Orthodox Christian from Bartella, on the Nineveh Plain. He and his wife had been living hand to mouth as displaced persons in Erbil since the outset of the ISIS invasion. In 2017, his wife had given birth to a baby boy, and at that time, Noor still had hopes that he would be able to return to his home in Bartella. He was an engineer by training and had been a teacher in Bartella before 2014. But he had not worked since then, and his salary from the government had stopped.

When the first planning for Christian returns and reconstruction in Nineveh were being developed through the Nineveh Reconstruction Committee (NRC), Noor had been chosen by the Syriac Orthodox Church to be one of their representatives. The NRC had been formed in 2016 as a working coalition of the major Christian churches of Nineveh in order to coordinate and support the return of the displaced Christians to the region. As an NRC representative, Noor had worked diligently for over a year to assess the damage to homes in Bartella and their rehabilitation needs, going through the structures one by one and making detailed reports, all without pay.

In January of 2017, I began making regular visits to Bartella, often accompanied by Noor. The town had seen heavy fighting and suffered serious damage during the ISIS war. Most buildings along the main frontage road of the town were flattened or blasted and shot through beyond repair. Inside all the churches, both Orthodox and Catholic, the interiors had been burned out and every Christian symbol either shot to pieces or hacked off and crushed with sledgehammers. But this desecration was mild in comparison to what had taken place in the main Orthodox cemetery just outside the church of Mar Shmony.

In the Syriac Orthodox tradition, the coffins of the deceased were not always buried in the earth. Instead they were often placed in family vaults made of stone which were semi-subterranean, with a foot or two showing above ground. There was a small, sealed entranceway dug into the ground to allow for additional coffins to be placed into the vault over time. Seeking to both desecrate and also steal whatever valuables might have been buried with the deceased, ISIS had forced open all of the vaults and smashed open the coffins.

Walking through the cemeteries, we looked through the now-open vaults and photographed the macabre scene. In many vaults, cinder blocks had been used to smash the lids of the coffins and expose the decomposed, skeletal remains inside. In others, the coffins had been dumped on their sides, the bodies lay in crumbling, decaying heaps on the floor. In one, an unused rocket had been used as a battering ram to force open a more solidly-built coffin.

As we walked from one vault to the next, we became aware of what we thought at first were white bits of trash and debris on the ground until we stopped and took a closer look, realizing with a shock that this was not trash or debris, but human bone fragments bleached white in the sun to which they had been exposed for these past two years and more. Now seeing the scene for what it was, we slowly scanned the entire cemetery and realized that its grounds were littered every few yards with similar remains—skull fragments, ribs, and countless other bones smashed into bits. This was Bartella after ISIS.

Later that spring, in what we viewed as an apparently sincere effort at outreach from the UNDP, their director of the Regional Bureau for Arab States had agreed to host the members of the NRC at a high-level meeting at UN Headquarters in New York. We were intending to lay out plans for a new period of cooperation between the church-managed programs of the NRC and those of the UN. Noor was to have been the representative for the Syriac Orthodox Church. Despite the official nature of the intended visit, Noor's application for a visa to join the delegation's visit to New York was summarily denied by the interviewing officer at the US consulate in Erbil, with no explanation given. As for the outcome of the meetings in New York, the promised follow-up visits to Iraq from the UNDP director never came, and the initiative died, stillborn.

Though rightfully frustrated, Noor nevertheless continued in his work for the NRC, hoping that serious funding would, at some point, arrive and that, along with everything else, he might receive some pay for his work. He had a young family now to support, and yet he and his family had run out of money, living now only on charity from relatives and friends. Just before Christmas in 2017, I had been able to get several thousand dollars to him to convince him to stay on. He was smart, spoke fluent English, and worked hard. The NRC needed him for the project, and his community would need people like him to rebuild.

But, as with everything in Iraq, setback followed upon disruption followed upon delay. In Bartella, the new power faction of the 30th Shabak brigade, closely allied with the Badr organization and its Iranian backers, moved into the void. The Christians of Bartella, including the Syriac Catholic community under Fr. Benham Benokha, made their case to everyone who would listen, and many who would not. The window of opportunity for a full Christian return to the town was rapidly closing, and there was not another season, another budget cycle, that they would be able to survive. In the town, those few families that had returned had done so only because of government jobs which required their presence in the town, or those who owned businesses there. Nearly the entire remainder of families stayed put in their displaced situations, mostly in Erbil.

By April of 2018, for Noor, it was enough. He had no more money. The Church-run food programs were out of money. The dream of returning to a Christian Bartella was disappearing, but most of all, he was tired, and the last remaining embers of hope for return had been put out. He had been displaced for nearly four years of his young life, and he had stayed and worked and hoped, yet it was all coming to nothing. Now he had a young son, and he could feel the life being drained from inside him. For Noor, it was time. He had done all that could be asked of him, and within the month, he and his family would go. There was nothing more I could say to him. A man wanted a future for his family.

Within the month, Noor and his family, together with his parents, were living in a two-room apartment in a small city in central Turkey, a five-hour drive from any international airport. While the Turkish government was still accepting refugees from Iraq, they were controlling where in the country they could live and, by design, kept them far from any of the major cities and tourist centers. For Noor, he was one of the last families to be allowed entry. Shortly after his arrival, Turkey stopped accepting additional refugees.

He had been allowed into the country on a refugee asylum application, registered with the UN as a refugee seeking emigration, and given an ID card that would need to be renewed every six months. His family had an initial interview with the UNHCR, after which they had heard nothing. He was made aware of a UN program which provided some help for the needs of the disabled, but for him and his family, there was nothing. They had some small funds from family and friends and, at least in theory, his father's pension in Iraq, which with some work might possibly be forwarded to them there in Turkey.

There were no work prospects in the town for any of the Christians from Iraq. Work required a permit from the government and the ability to speak Turkish. Even with a permit, it was evident to them all that no Christians would be hired, and as a result, few even tried for a permit. Occasionally, the young men would be hired for cash as day laborers, but for most families, they were simply trapped and waiting.

Noor's was one of the few Syriac Orthodox families, with most of the Christian refugees being Chaldean. It was difficult to get an exact count on the number of families, as the population was transient, but it seemed there were several hundred there, with perhaps a population of one thousand people or more. There were no Christian churches of any kind. People met in private houses to share prayers and meditations. A Chaldean priest came twice a year, Christmas and Easter, and gave the sacraments to all Christians who came to him. He would give Masses and hear confessions, from morning through the night, in the packed homes and gathering places where the faithful stood patiently, the crowd spilling out the doors. No other priests came, and this was the totality of the Christian faith. For many, as the months wore on into years, although grateful for the visits of the priest and still deeply attached to their faith, they wondered where was their church and why was there not a greater presence or more help?

The schools that were available were all taught in Turkish, and a heavy Islamic element pervaded. The Christian refugees kept their children home and tried as best they could to give them some basic education. Everyone hoped to leave soon, and they could not see any point in learning Turkish, yet most of them had been there since 2014 already.

Noor had no hope for emigration to the US, especially after his experience with the visa denial in Erbil. For the Iraqi Christians, it had been accepted belief going back to the Obama administration that there was prejudice against Christians in the established international emigration process, not only from the US but carrying through to the predominantly Muslim local staffs of the UN and their migrant agency, the IOM. Despite an initial hope that this might change under the Trump administration, the Christians of Iraq had seen no improvement at all in terms of emigration to the US, and in fact, even those applications that had been far along in the process seemed all to have simply stopped where they were, with no notice or update.

Noor had family in Canada, and he hoped to go there. He had friends that hoped to go to Australia. Nearly all had given up on entry to the US. Perhaps the policy might change someday. A survey had been done by the Church to gather statistics as to where the Christian refugees preferred to go. Afterwards, discussing their preferences amongst their fellow refugees, they were surprised that so many of them had chosen the same destination: anywhere.

In August of 2019, Noor and his family were still in Turkey. He had his Turkish ID card and his Iraqi passport, which he dreaded to show anywhere for fear of the automatic response—"terrorist." He longed for an identity that would give him stability instead of suspicion, a life where he could stay in one place and build a home.

He spoke, from time to time, by VOIP with his friends from Bartella who were still in Iraq. I reached him this way in the summer of 2019, just as this book was being finished. I asked him if he knew anybody in the Christian refugee community from Bartella who would consider returning to Iraq.

"There is nobody who will return. Even now, I can tell you there are no Christians still in Iraq who want to be in Bartella. The only Christians there now are the people who have a government job and have to be there, or people who own a business that they need to take care of because they have no money otherwise. The others will all stay in Erbil. The situation in Bartella is dangerous for the Christians. This is seriously dangerous from these *Hashd* people now after these last weeks. This is dangerous for you also, seriously dangerous, and you should not go there anymore."

The "Hashd" people were the 30th Shabak Brigade, one of the many paramilitary units which formed in the aftermath of the ISIS takeover of Nineveh in 2014 and would later collectively become known as the *Hashd Al Sha'abi*, or Popular Mobilization Units. During the ISIS war, formal steps were taken by the Iraqi government to incorporate these units into the Iraqi military and security structure. By the end of 2017, there were calls for the *Hashd Al Sha'abi* units to fully integrate into the Iraqi army, but the armed militias proved unwilling in many cases to surrender the territories they now controlled. From the failure of the Iraqi government to firmly take control of the situation then came the growing assertion of power by the paramilitary units over the next two years. As many of the units were Shia, with close support from Iran, the *Hashd Al Sha'abi* would increasingly become a means of Iranian proxy control over territories inside Iraq.

Allied with the Iranian-backed Babylon Brigade and the Badr Organization, the 30th Shabak brigade, formed as the *Qawat Sahl Ninawa*, was comprised mainly of Shabak fighters originally intent on recovering Nineveh from ISIS. Although not strictly Muslim, the Shabak had formed an alliance with Shia Iran and sought to remain separate from either Kurdish or Sunni Arab domination in Iraq. To the ISIS fighters, the Shabak were heretics and were considered rightful targets for murder and genocide. In returning to their historical homes throughout Nineveh Province, the Shabak, and the 30th, were seeking a new stronghold.

While initially the Christians held out some hope that, in their shared experience as victims of genocide at the hands of ISIS, Shabak leaders might seek peaceful coexistence with their Christian neighbors, the push and support of their Iranian backers soon put any such promise aside. Instead, in the aftermath of the war, the 30th became little more than an armed gang seeking to impose control over the Christian towns in which it held a foothold, and their primary target became the town of Bartella.

Engaging rapidly in a pattern of intimidation and control within the town, the members of the 30th set up roadblocks and checkpoints to prevent free movement of people attempting to return and rebuild. Christian families were threatened into selling their homes, and many began to give up on ever returning to the town. Public demonstrations and pleas from the church leaders drew only passing sympathy and slight recognition in the West. Promised rebuilding projects from the UN barely arrived and, when they did, were continued in the lamentable pattern of sham presentations. Having set an amount of $2,000 per home as the fixed rehabilitation amount, the UNDP sent in non-Christian contractors to the Christian homes, who repainted and refinished one or two downstairs rooms, then called the work complete while the kitchens and bathrooms remained unusable, gutted second floors remained untouched, and windows and doors blown out and open to the elements.

Later, in 2018, the German government would belatedly begin to place some focus on the critical importance of rebuilding the homes of the minorities in Nineveh if there was any hope of maintaining the ancient cultural pluralism that had existed there for nearly two millennia. In a well-intentioned plan to be implemented on the ground through the highly regarded German NGO, Malteser International, the German government had authorized the initial spending of over 10 million Euros specifically for the restoration of homes, including those in Bartella. But once again, a strict adherence to "process," imposed on Malteser by the government decision makers in Berlin, thwarted the intent.

In this case, one of the qualifiers for receiving funds from the German project was that the homes could not have been worked on previously by the UNDP. When pressed on the issue, it became clear the reason for this was that to go back and perform additional work on homes that the UNDP had earlier "repaired" would indicate that the UN contractors had not properly done their job, and the German government in Berlin would not do this. In a private discussion after one meeting between the German representatives and the church leaders from the towns of Nineveh, the Germans on site frankly admitted, with apparent personal frustration, that their government would not "embarrass" the UN in this way.

For the Christians of Bartella, who had been recipients months earlier of the sham repairs performed by UNDP contractors, the exclusion from this additional help, which might allow them to actually inhabit their homes, was fundamentally and morally unjust, and they were enraged. They were victims of genocide trying to rebuild their lives. How could they be used again and again by the Western governments whose policy failures and aid paradigms had played such a heavy role in their ongoing misery? Fr. Benham Benokha of the Syriac Catholic Church in Bartella said to me at the time, "They do not care. We will disappear here, and they will just want to show in their reports that they have protected their money and they have completed their projects according to their plans. That is all. They do not care about what actually happens to the people. They do not care."

From that point on, the strangulation of Bartella by the Shabak 30th and its cohorts continued to increase. Ironically, in what history will likely view as a tragically late, if well-intentioned, show of seriousness by the US, the matter was brought to a tipping point for the Iraqi government and for the affected minorities of Nineveh. Having moved since 2014 in a pattern of agonizing slowness and indifference to the immediacy of the issue, with most actions taken having been misdirected and then misapplied, the US finally began to take steps demonstrating some clarity of purpose.

Throughout 2018, as the Trump administration began to slowly put its own people in place, the logistical and planning issues of minority returns to Nineveh, primarily Christians and Yazidis, began to establish some footholds of priority. Acting upon the public words of the Iraqi government, as repeatedly and publicly voiced by their ambassador to the US, Fareed Yasseen, that "Iraq without its minorities is not Iraq,"[1] the US threw their support into a plan of stabilizing Nineveh through the removal of all paramilitary units and replacing them with a federal police force controlled by the central government in Baghdad and manned by personnel indigenous to the region.

For months throughout 2018 and then in to 2019, the US pressured the central government in Baghdad and the Kurdish government in Erbil that this was the only way to move forward. The US analysis was that the continued presence of armed militias loyal only to their own power faction, which in the case of many of the units also meant Iran, was prohibitive to the peace and stability necessary for rebuilding. Moreover, made clear by the US representatives, the specific cases of both the 30th Shabak brigade and the 50th Babylon Brigade, were a threshold obstacle to long-term US support for the rehabilitation of the region. In a private meeting with Christian leaders in Erbil, Max Primorac, special envoy for Vice President Pence, said, "We have made it clear to both Baghdad and Erbil that they need to make a choice. They can have the full backing of the United States to restore these towns with long-term support from us, or they can choose to be a colony of Iran, but if they choose the latter, the US will not be paying for it and they will be on their own. The government of Iraq will then have to face its own people and take ownership of its choices."

In calling for the removal of the militias, the US position was consistent with the strong public stance which had been taken by the Chaldean Church since the beginning of the returns to Nineveh in 2016. In Baghdad, His Beatitude Patriarch Louis Sako had made repeated

---

1 Statement by Iraqi Ambassador to US, Fareed Yaseen, "Reconstructing Iraq: Challenges Ahead," *The Hudson Institute*, February 22, 2018, accessed October, 2019, https://www.youtube.com/watch?time_continue=4828&v=Hgy18S1oiLE.

statements that the Church supported Christian men signing up to take proper responsibility in the security and protection of Nineveh, but that if they wished to do so, they should join the properly established military for their region, which meant either joining the Iraqi army or the Peshmerga. The Church, said the Patriarch, was formally and firmly against any Christian militia forces. In Erbil, Archbishop Bashar Warda continued this position. In his many international speaking engagements during this period, whenever asked about the establishment of a Christian militia, his rhetorical response would always be the same—something along the lines of: "In the history of the Middle East, show me one occasion in which a group received arms and did not eventually use them against another for aggressive purposes. We Christians are a people of peace here in Iraq. We are the one group that has not used violence against any other. If we are to independently arm ourselves now and form our own militia, sooner or later we will shoot at somebody in aggression, and then what is there to separate us from any other of these gangs? What moral ground will we be standing on then?"

In the months that followed, the weakness of the central government in Baghdad became clear, as did the apparent strength of the Iranian tentacles which were slowly strangling much of the country. Despite repeated announcements from Baghdad regarding ever-shifting deadlines for the departure of the *Hashd Al-Sha'abi* units from the checkpoints and towns, nothing effectively changed. Moreover, in the delays, concerns grew daily that the *Hashd* units and their Iranian-influenced supporters were simply stalling in order to put into place structures that would allow for any change in control, aside from the *Hashd*, to simply be a matter of show. The *Hashd* members would simply exchange their existing uniforms for new Iraqi federal uniforms, with the men and power structures still intact. For the Christians in the impacted towns, they openly feared that this type of forced surface change would ultimately give their tormentors even greater authority and cover to continue their behavior. Even more alarming, repeated reports began circulating that Iranian-influenced actors had gained control of the passport control office in Mosul, and that valid Iraqi passports were now being issued, in the thousands, to Iranian fighting men who would then be in position to be given priority in the creation of any new federal security force in northern Iraq. By the spring of 2019, most consular and international security staff were privately admitting these reports were likely true.

Then, in July of 2019, seeking both to increase the pressure on the Iraqi central government and also to show the seriousness of the US position, the US Treasury Department's Office of Foreign Assets Control (OFAC) announced formal sanctions against four Iraqi nationals, including the leader of the 30th Shabak Brigade, Waad Qado, and also the nominal Christian front man for the 50th Babylon Brigade, Rayan Al-Kildani. In the accompanying press release posted on the Treasury Department website on July 18, 2019, the charges read out against the actors were as follows:

> Many of the corruption and abuse-related actions committed by these sanctioned individuals occurred in areas where persecuted religious communities are struggling to recover from the horrors inflicted on them by ISIS. Therefore, today's sanctions demonstrate solidarity with all Iraqis who oppose corruption and human rights abuse undertaken by public officials, and underscore the Administration's commitment to support the recovery of persecuted religious communities in Iraq.
>
> As a result of today's actions, all property and interests in property of these individuals, and any entities that are owned, directly or indirectly, 50 percent or more by these individuals, that are in the United States or in the possession or control of U.S. persons must be blocked and reported to OFAC. OFAC's regulations generally prohibit any dealings by U.S. persons or within (or transiting) the United States that involve any property or interests in property of blocked persons.

RAYAN AL-KILDANI

> Rayan al-Kildani (al-Kildani) was designated for being a foreign person who is responsible for or complicit in, or who has directly or indirectly engaged in, serious human rights abuse.
>
> Al-Kildani is the leader of the 50th Brigade militia. In May 2018, a video circulated among Iraqi human rights civil society organizations in which al-Kildani cut off the ear of a handcuffed detainee.

The 50th Brigade is reportedly the primary impediment to the return of internally displaced persons to the Ninewa Plain. The 50th Brigade has systematically looted homes in Batnaya, which is struggling to recover from ISIS's brutal rule. The 50th Brigade has reportedly illegally seized and sold agricultural land, and the local population has accused the group of intimidation, extortion, and harassment of women.

WAAD QADO

Waad Qado (Qado) was designated for being a foreign person who is or has been a leader or official of an entity, including any government entity, that has engaged in, or whose members have engaged in, serious human rights abuse relating to the leader's or official's tenure.

Qado is the leader of the 30th Brigade militia. The 30th Brigade has extracted money from the population around Bartalla, in the Ninewa Plain, through extortion, illegal arrests, and kidnappings. The 30th Brigade has frequently detained people without warrants, or with fraudulent warrants, and has charged arbitrary customs fees at its checkpoints. Members of the local population allege that the 30th Brigade has been responsible for egregious offenses including physical intimidation, extortion, robbery, kidnapping, and rape.

The immediate reaction amongst the Christian communities of Iraq was a mix of satisfaction and apprehension.

On the one hand, these were truly bad men. Although they had both played a role, however debatable in its importance, in the defeat of ISIS in the region, they had also immediately then settled into an overt power grab in their areas.

For Rayan Al-Kildani, a Chaldean Christian from Al-Qosh by birth, but who had long since been reputed to have left his faith for a role with Shia- and Iranian-linked power factions, his position as leader of the Babylon Brigade served to give it the cynical cover of a "Christian" militia protecting the interests of the persecuted Christian minorities in Telkayf and northern Nineveh province. In reality, his men were nearly all Shia, many from Iran or the south of Iraq. At one point, feeling pressure to provide better cover for their alleged status as a Christian militia, the 50th had attempted to recruit displaced Christians in the south who were mostly without work and destitute, offering them paid positions within the Babylon Brigade if they would come north and join them. But the reputation of the 50th as a front organization for Iran and the Shia was too widely known, and his recruiters came back essentially empty-handed. At the same time, wanting to shore up his fighting strength, Kildani looked to the former ISIS fighters then in quasi-hiding in and around the former ISIS stronghold of Telkayf, a town now firmly under the thumb of the 50th Babylon. Many of them battle-hardened fighters desperate for money and protection, the once hard-line anti-Shia terrorists now rallied to them as a flag of convenience.

Meanwhile in the towns controlled by the 50th, the grab for control and money from rehabilitation funds went forward. In a US State Department-funded cash-for-work program in Batnaya, the locally-hired female manager found herself threatened by the local henchman of Kildani, who alternatively made sexual advances against her and threatened her, demanding that she put only Kildani-affiliated people on the work list, including phantom positions for himself and his son. Informed about the threats, the State Department representative in Erbil shut the Batnaya program down.

As for Kildani, his brutality was by then widely acknowledged in the region. The existence of the video referenced in the OFAC sanction release was an open secret in Nineveh, and many copies of it had been circulating since the fall of 2016. In it, a man alleged to be Kildani is shown facing the camera and leaning into the bed of a pickup truck in which several men are sitting, hands and feet bound behind their backs and eyes and mouths covered with cloth strips tied behind their heads. The prisoners are all dressed in white and alleged to be ISIS fighters or sympathizers taken by Kildani's men in the town of Telkayf in November of 2016. Reaching into the bed of the truck and over to the prisoner closest to him, Kildani grabs his right ear in one hand and, with the other hand, reaches in with a six-inch knife and, with several heavy slices, pulls off the ear of the helpless prisoner, holding the piece of flesh up and waving it clearly for all to see.

While the public international sanctioning and shaming of the two *Hashd* commanders drew immediate applause from all those who had suffered at their hands, both Muslim and Christian alike, when I asked an Iraqi Christian friend what he thought, he was cautious, even skeptical. "Wait ten days," he said. "We need to see what follows."

And in Iraq, something always followed.

The first pushback came from the followers of Kildani in the week following the sanctions. Acting on information allegedly put forward by undisclosed sources, Kildani's people began denouncing the Chaldean archbishop of Erbil, Bashar Warda, in social media within Iraq as being the source of the information used by the Americans to sanction Kildani. In truth, while the Church and the archbishop had long advocated publicly for the removal of all paramilitary units, they had otherwise strived to maintain a prudent neutrality, often under tremendous pressure from all sides, including frequently the Americans themselves. But for Kildani's people, the intended implication was clear—the archbishop and, by extension, the Church, were in league with the Americans against the *Hashd* and therefore, in the minds of the *Hashd*, against the people of Iraq. Although Erbil, as the capital of the Kurdistan Region and therefore well outside any *Hashd*-controlled areas, provided nominal safety against potential *Hashd* related reprisals there, the situation appeared to be deteriorating rapidly, and alliances and trust were increasingly unsteady.

A month earlier, at the inauguration ceremony in Erbil for the new Kurdistan Region president, Nichirvan Barzani, Kildani had been an honored guest and provided with a front-row seat. Faced with a furious reaction from the US government, the Kurds backtracked and attempted to claim that Kildani's presence had been a protocol mix-up, that the Kurds had been given no clear notice as to who would be coming as part of the Baghdad delegation. But photos from the welcome carpet of the event showing Barzani and Kildani warmly embracing each other and speaking at length seemed to belie any confusion. The moment passed, but the import was clear—everyone was hedging now and nothing was certain. The rising specter of conflict between the US and Iran had, by now, colored everything, and the US pullout of its non-critical staff from the embassy in Baghdad and the consulate in Erbil on May 15th had placed a pall over every relationship in Iraq. The looming question for all sides in Iraq was how far the US would actually go. How deep was the commitment to actually force the Iranians out of Iraq?

For the 30th Shabak Brigade in Bartella, they had guessed that the US commitment was not deep enough to force them out, and neither was the Iraqi Federal government's ability or inclination to help. By late July, *Hashd* had influenced social media in Bartella and the region had begun calling out Fr. Thabet of Karemlesh in similar fashion to the accusations made a week earlier against Archbishop Warda. Public demonstrations in Bartella were widely covered in Iraqi media showing mobs of Shabak supporters of the 30th desecrating the American flag and accusing the Christians of being together with the Americans in assaulting the sovereignty of Iraq. The danger was becoming very real, and for the Christians, they waited with increasing concern to see what follow-up would be coming from both the Americans and the federal government in Baghdad.

Throughout the second half of July, I had been forwarding along pertinent clips from Iraqi media, including widely-viewed social media, to appropriate people within the Trump administration, USAID, the State Department, and Congress. I urged them to understand the seriousness of the situation for the Christians of northern Iraq and the importance of follow-through. The Christians were once again being exposed, and while they continued to support the removal of the paramilitary units, they had expected it to be done in a way that did not recklessly leave them in harm's way, having to bear the brunt of an anger which they had not themselves stirred.

From the other end of calls in Washington, DC, came variations of the same theme. It was now with the Iraqi government to show their colors. They had repeatedly promised to remove the *Hashd* elements, and their deadlines were upon them. We had told them clearly that continued US aid depended upon removing themselves from under Iran. If the Iraqis could not show that they intended to hold up their end of the relationship, this might be the point at which the US pivot away from supporting a return to Nineveh begins to take place. But what about the Christians left in the middle, I asked, what is the plan for them? Would the US consider pivoting its support to helping the Christians rebuild in the relative safety surrounding Erbil? The best answer received was that this might be possible and that perhaps it would be considered.

Meanwhile, from DOD and the senior offices of the State Department, the word was coming back that the major issue was now preventing the resurgence of ISIS and the resolution of conflict in Syria. The issue of the Christians of Nineveh was not deemed critical—the US had done their part to give the Iraqi government an opportunity to show that they legitimately cared about their own minorities, and now it was up to them to prove it. The US had spent hundreds of millions of dollars trying to revive Nineveh, but the Iraqi government needed to get on board now, or the US would start to climb off. One thing was becoming clear—within the US, it seemed unlikely that there was any plan B in the works for the Christians.

A person with regular access to the administration, who was also a close friend and supporter of the Christian cause in Iraq, called me in the midst of these days and relayed a conversation he had just had with a senior policy member of the administration involved in the Iraq issue.

"I was pretty blunt with him," my friend said. "I told him that in launching these sanctions they had put all their money on red, and if this came up black, the Christians will pay the price, and they could get hurt badly for it, maybe for good."

"You're right," the other had answered. "I know, and you are right."

For the 30th Shabak Brigade, they were calling bluff to the whole matter. In early August, their supporters blocked the main road into and out of northern Nineveh, effectively sealing off the towns of Karemlesh, Qaraqosh, and Bartella in protest of the federal government's order for the *Hashd* of the 30th to leave the checkpoints. At the same time, three Russian-made tanks were delivered to the 30th from the Iraqi army, and media showed them being offloaded from flatbeds and rumbling over to take up positions just three miles outside Bartella. The Christians, including Fr. Thabet in Karemlesh, increasingly alarmed and expecting a response from Baghdad, stayed quiet and remained in their towns.

The response from Baghdad showed the Shabak had guessed right, at least for the moment. Sent up as negotiators to deal with the Shabak militia, were Faleh al Fayad, the formal head in Baghdad of the *Hashd Al-Shaabi* units and National Security Advisor to the Prime Minister, and Abu Mahdi al Muhandis, Deputy Head of the *Hashd Al-Shaabi* units for all of Iraq with direct reporting to the Prime Minister. The two met directly with the Shabak leaders only, and did not meet with any members of the Christian leadership. On the departure of the negotiators from Baghdad, the 30th Brigade still held the checkpoints, the three Russian tanks remained parked outside Bartella, and the Shabak supporters of the *Hashd* jubilantly claimed victory over the Americans and the Christians, to which the federal government in Baghdad issued no response.

As Noor said on the phone days later, nobody will go back there now. Seriously, for Christians, it is dangerous.

* * *

FOR NOOR'S FORMER NEIGHBORS FROM BARTELLA, now elsewhere in the diaspora, things may have been no longer dangerous, but they were hardly sustainable. A friend living in a crowded two-room apartment in Amman, Jordan, survived on the remnants of savings and day labor for cash. He had registered his family with UNHCR as refugees on their arrival from Iraq in 2015, but his case had seen no progress since. Living with only an ID card from UNHCR and his Iraqi passport, he was prohibited by the Jordanian government from any regular employment. There were no schools available for the children, but there was both an Orthodox and Catholic church nearby, and their faith had remained strong. He and his wife spoke with friends still back in Iraq frequently, but they had no thoughts of ever returning to Iraq. As for where they would go, they too would go anywhere.

In Lebanon, the story was much the same. Noor's friend there, also from Bartella, headed a family of six now living in a three-room apartment with no money left other than what could be earned from day labor. Regular employment was prohibited for refugees, and five Christians had been put in jail in the past few months for misrepresenting their status in order to get work. Their family had come to Lebanon directly in the fall of 2014, not waiting to see what might take place in Iraq. For them, they were finished with Iraq and there was nothing that could bring them back. And yet, although they had registered with UNHCR immediately upon their arrival in Lebanon, nearly five years later they were still waiting for an immigration slot to open up for them—anywhere. As for their faith, they were fortunate. They lived in a

Christian area and had easy access to a church. They were able to go to Mass every week still, and their faith remained strong.

* * *

"HOW CAN WE STAY IN SYRIA?" the young engineer asked me.

It was early winter in 2017, and he had arrived in Erbil the week before with his wife, mother, and young daughter. He was from Aleppo, and his home there had been destroyed in August 2012 as the fighting there raged between the Syrian army and the opposition forces. His father had been one of the more than 10,000 civilians killed in the cross-fire. Since then, his family had moved seven times trying to stay ahead of the conflict, twice fleeing just ahead of the arrival of Islamist units.

"This fighting will not stop," he continued. "Assad will win this war, but not completely, and this fighting will not stop. The Christians will be with him. They have no choice. Many of the Muslims are with ISIS and the others like them. Many, many, many. The leaders of the churches are all with Assad. They have no choice. But this fighting will return. The Christians will be in the middle. Please, can you find me some work?"

The Syrian Christians, by then, were beginning to appear in Erbil daily, and none of them had plans to return to their home country. At the time of the civil war outbreak of 2011, the Christian population of Syria was estimated by most counts to be as much as 10 percent of an overall population of just over 20 million. By 2017, reliable numbers for the remaining Christians were impossible to reach, but most estimates were that more than half of the Christians had fled the country.

As the civil war slowly ground down and the Assad government regained control, the Christians still remaining began to rebuild. But for the Christians there, the situation was significantly different from the one facing the Iraqi Christians. In Iraq, the West and the Christian leaders themselves, supported developing a close integration of the remaining Christian population with the Iraqi federal government. In Syria, the government was led by Bashar Al Assad, a man viewed by Western governments as a ruthless dictator, a sponsor of terrorism and crimes against humanity and an international pariah. But for Western private aid organizations wishing to help the churches there, the often-public alliance being shown by the Christians with Assad posed a myriad of problems with their own country's compliance laws. The Christian leaders in Syria, meanwhile, had been forced into a position of aligning, however tenuously, with Assad as their protector against the constantly evolving Islamist elements of the opposition forces.

In the course of the civil war, these Islamist elements, including ISIS, had waged the same horrific violence against Christians as had been seen in Iraq, driving the Christians either to flee the country or move under the comparative protection of the Assad regime.

We had found work for the engineer later that winter. He was hardworking, and his English was nearly fluent. A year later, I saw him at a work site, and we spoke. The situation in Syria was settling down. I asked, would he ever think about returning?

"Never," he said. "This violence there will not stop, and the Christians will pay a price for staying with Assad. Maybe not today, but in the future. ISIS and this mentality will not go away. It is no place for me and my family."

He was registered with the UNHCR and was hoping someday to go to Canada or the US. He did not want to go to Europe anymore. He feared the situation there—the rising Islamist element on one side, the native backlash on the other. He had friends in Germany and France. None of the native people there think of us as Christians, they had told him. We are all Arabs to them.

CHAPTER 10

The Salt of the Earth

"They will kill this child," the bishop said.

I looked at him.

"Yes," the other older priest nodded. "They will put the child in a bag of rocks and throw it in the river or kill it some other way." He waved his hand toward me in a backhanded motion.

"Then I have your permission?" I asked.

"Yes, do what you must. Be careful. Protect the Church as best you can, but save the child."

Even now, nearly three years later, I hesitate to tell the story. We have kept it all secret, everyone involved. But as I look back, I cannot escape it. If there was ever a story that showed why the Christian presence still had meaning, what our witness could still mean, it was this.

In my telling of it now, the names and locations and other details must be left out, not only for the protection of the actors, but more importantly for the child, who survived and is safe and loved and has known nothing in its young life other than the family it is now with.

The story began in Washington, DC, where the wife of a congressman had a friend who knew a missionary who had information about a child that was four weeks from being born. The mother of the child was barely fourteen and had been raped daily for months while captive as an

ISIS sex slave. She had managed to escape but was pregnant now. She was not Christian, and the elders in her community would take the child when it was born and kill it. The child-mother did not want it killed and, through a cousin, got word that she wanted help to another friend, who contacted the missionary, who contacted the congressman's wife, whose staff contacted me. Would the Catholic Church in the Middle East be able to help?

A week later, I had run down the particulars. We had been living then for over a year with the dust of blown-up towns on our boots and the smell of burned-out homes in our senses. We worked and wandered through these towns now as if it were the natural state of things; why would towns not have bomb craters? We were in many ways numbed to personal tragedy—everybody had one. So, when the girl's intermediary finally stood before us asking if we could help, our answer was yes, perhaps, but why us? And the answer came back and stopped us, for just a moment at least.

"The mother wants the child to live," the intermediary began. She looked at us with the fear and confusion of an uneducated woman in wartime taking a risk with people she did not know.

"She knows that you are Christians, and you will not kill the child."

The mind reels.

I have seen the child since, but only in pictures. By design, I know nothing of the family that ultimately took in the child, other than that they willingly took in the infant as their own and have since made it out of Iraq safely to a new life in a new country. Of the sisters and priests who took all the risks and protected the child until a home could be found, they are who and what I choose to think of these days when I think of the Catholic Church in action. Perhaps someday their full story may be told, but I very much doubt any of them would wish it so. The child's survival and ultimate escape was our small miracle, and in that miracle was recognition enough.

* * *

"WE ARE ALL MUSLIMS."

On the TV screen inside the rectory in Erbil we watched as the protestors, thousands of miles away in the US, held up their signs and banners protesting the Trump administration travel restrictions on several countries around the world, restrictions that much of the West reflexively viewed as anti-Muslim. Ironically, the restrictions had also just prevented the intended visit to the US of the Catholic archbishop of Erbil, Bashar Warda, where he was scheduled to speak on the plight of Christians in Iraq.

Meanwhile, the protestors in the US, many of them young students from elite universities, shouted obscenities in one verse while chanting solidarity with "oppressed" Muslims in another. Their belief was that the travel ban was "Islamophobic" in design and purpose, and the proper remedy for the West was to show solidarity with those who were, in their view, oppressed and suffering from this unjust prejudice.

Fr. Samir, a priest from Shaqlawa—a once historic Christian enclave with its Christian presence since run over and all but completely extinguished by a wave of Arab Muslim migration from the south caused by the unending decades of war—looked at the TV screen and shook his head, then turned towards me questioningly.

"Tell me, brother, when all of our people were being chased from their homes and killed and tortured and forced to live as homeless people, and the doors of all the Western countries stayed closed to us, did any of these people wear shirts or protest or hold signs that said, 'We are all Christians'?"

The answer, of course, was no. But why so?

Certainly, the growing secularism of the West and its related antipathy, even hostility, to the Christian faith played a major role. Christianity's role as a dominant social force over the last millennia had made it among the leading targets for criticism and blame for society's ills, whether legitimate or not. And within that analysis, the seemingly never-ending disclosures of abuse within the Roman Catholic Church made it particularly easy to be scorned, certainly not any object of sympathy. Yet in this, the Christians of the East were innocent. They had been acknowledged by the Obama administration as victims of genocide. Why then were they not worthy of some sympathy and compassion from those screaming for social justice on seemingly every other front?

Over the course of the prior years, I had heard many explanations for this, but it was put to me most succinctly by an Anglican layman who had been indefatigable in advocating in the UK and EU regarding the plight of Christians in the Middle East. We were sitting in the basement cafeteria of the Supreme Court of the UK in London on March 22, 2017, preparing for presentations and meetings to be held the next day at the UK House of Lords. I had come to know this man as person of wisdom and long views, and I put the question to him as we finished our work—why was the plight of the Christians of the East never a concern in the West?

"Worldliness," he said to me in a manner of both resignation and frustration. "The educated West is only concerned with showing its own worldliness and sophistication, and you don't do this by showing support for Christians. It's simply not fashionable."

Fifteen minutes later, as I stepped outside onto the street with the communications director for the UK Office of Aid to Church in Need, a police car screeched to a stop and made a violent U-turn in the direction of Parliament, sirens blaring and lights flashing. We looked around, and it was clear that we had just stepped into a world of security mayhem. We headed quickly away from the seeming direction of activity and stepped into a coffee shop where the TV screen was reporting on a developing incident involving an attack at Westminster. Hours later, we would learn the full story regarding a fifty-two-year-old convert to Islam who had intentionally run down and killed four people, injuring dozens of others outside the Palace of Westminster, then jumping out and stabbing to death an unarmed police officer before being shot dead by security officers.

I had been scheduled, along with several others, to speak the next day, March 23rd, before the House of Lords regarding the status of the displaced Christians of Iraq, but following the attacks of the day before, the entire Parliament had been shut down to all outside visitors due to security measures. The hearing was to be chaired, however, by Lord David Alton of Liverpool, who had other thoughts as to the appropriateness of cancelling the hearing and arranged for special permission for me to come in alone and speak. As he would later write in a commentary in the UK *Catholic Herald*, "Mr. Rasche's visit comes at a critical time in the wake of the expulsion of ISIS from the Nineveh Plains, the region of northern Iraq which for centuries has been home to Catholic and Orthodox communities as well as other minorities. What sort of message would it have sent to them if that meeting had to be cancelled because of Islamist terror on the streets of London?"[1]

Later that day, in a follow-up meeting of the larger group of advocates, I listened to the Egyptian Coptic Archbishop Angaelos speak to the rest of us about the language being used to counter seemingly every nascent attempt to specifically recognize the reality of the persecution of Middle Eastern Christians by Middle Eastern Muslims. Inevitably, the counter claim that would eventually be hurled at us in any public forums for discussion concerning the plight of Christians reached one word—Islamophobia. But what then of the never-ending violence that was factually taking place against Christians?

In the years that followed, Bishop Angaelos would become one of the leading proponents of a the effort to address the persecution of Christians in the East and around the world, and the acceptance of that persecution by much of the fashionable and worldly West, for what it was—Christophobia. In widely-circulated comments, Bishop Angaelos wrote, "It has been my belief that while there is no recognized term to express anti-Christian sentiment and violence, attacks will remain in the hearts and minds of observers as sporadic and unrelated incidents. As with other patterns of targeting and demonizing, it is equally undeniable that there is a trend, and an escalating phenomenon, that increasingly leads to Christians being targeted, attacked and even murdered for merely affirming and living their Faith." Writing further, he argued, "While there is increasing awareness and focus on the unacceptable and undeniable growth of anti-Semitism, Islamophobia and Xenophobia, it is also essential for us, at the same time, to understand and recognize the increasing trend of hostility and targeted attacks on Christians around the world."[2]

---

[1] David Alton, "Westminster has seen worse. Now it must show persecuted Christians that terror won't win." *The Catholic Herald,* March 23, 2017, accessed October, 2019, https://catholicherald.co.uk/commentandblogs/2017/03/23/westminster-has-seen-worse-now-it-must-show-persecuted-christians-that-terror-wont-win.

[2] Archbishop Cranmer, "Coptic Archbishop Angaelos says Christophobia is an 'escalating phenomenon'," *archbishopcranmer.com,* March 7, 2019, accessed October, 2019, https://archbishopcranmer.com/coptic-archbishop-angaelos-christophobia/.

In a defiant, closely-followed speech sponsored by the Religious Freedom Project at Georgetown University, the predecessor organization to the highly-respected Religious Freedom Institute on Capitol Hill, given in February of 2018, Archbishop Warda of Erbil went directly at the issue without apology.[3]

Following more than 1900 years of existence in Mesopotamia, we Christians of Iraq now find ourselves on the very edge of extinction. From a land where our martyrs' blood nourished the earliest flowering of our faith, our Church contributed to carrying the Good News as far away as India and China. Our Christian ancestors shared with Muslim Arabs a deep tradition of thought and philosophy and engaged with them in dialogue respectfully since the 8th century AD. The Arabic Golden Age, historian Philip Jenkins has noted, was built on Chaldean and Syriac scholarship. Now we face the end in Iraq, the same end faced by the Iraqi Jews before us, and the same end now being faced by the Yazidis, with whom we have suffered so much pain, alongside us. We Christians, a people who have endured persecution in patience and faith for 1,400 years, now confront an existential struggle. It is possibly the last struggle we will confront in Iraq.

The most immediate cause is the ISIS attacks that led to the displacement of more than 125,000 Christians from our historical homelands and rendered us, in a single night, without shelter and refuge, without work or properties, without churches and monasteries, without the ability to participate in any of the things which give one a life of dignity: family visits, celebration of weddings and births, the sharing of sorrows. Our tormentors confiscated our present while also seeking to wipe out our history and destroy our future.

And yet we are still there. Scourged, battered, and wounded. Yet still there. And having survived thus far, to this point of near finality,

---

3 Bashar Warda, "The Future of Religious Pluralism in Iraq," speech hosted by the Religious Freedom Research Project of Georgetown University's Berkley Center for Religion, Peace, and World Affairs, April 12, 2018, accessed October, 2019, https://www.religiousfreedominstitute.org/blog/ archbishop-bashar-warda-the-future-of-religious-pluralism-in-iraq?rq=Bashar%20Warda.

we have been granted a position of clarity and courage that we have perhaps lacked, or avoided, up until this day. We can no longer ignore the fundamental cause of what has been a relentless persecution of our people for a nearly a millennium and half. Having faced for 1,400 years a slow-motion genocide that began long before the ongoing ISIS genocide today, the time for excusing this inhuman behavior and its causes is long since past.

When a people have nothing left to lose, in some sense it is very liberating, and from this position of clarity and new-found courage, I must speak to you honestly on behalf of my people and speak to you the truth. The truth is that there is a fundamental crisis within Islam itself and if this crisis is not acknowledged, addressed, and fixed then there can be no future for Christians or any other form of religious plurality in the Middle East. Indeed, there is little reason to see a future for anyone in the Middle East, including within the Muslim world itself, other than in the context of continued violence, revenge, and hatred. And as we have seen too many times, this violence seeks to overtake us all, and destroy vulnerable innocent lives wherever it can find them.

Prior to the ISIS horror of 2014, we Iraqi Christians had historically endeavored to maintain a dialogue of life with Muslims. In this dialogue we refrained from speaking honestly and truthfully to our oppressors in order to simply survive and live quietly. We would not openly face the long history of violence and murder inflicted upon us. We did not push back against the constantly recurring periods of extremism that inflicted such pain and violence against the innocents, both Muslim and Christian alike. But following the horror of ISIS there is nothing left for us now but to speak plainly and unreservedly: there is a crisis of violence in Islam and for the sake of humanity, including the followers of Islam themselves, it must be addressed openly and honestly.

At the root of all of this we must be straightforward about the reality of the teachings of *Jihad*, which are the justification for all these acts of violence. Apologists for the history of the last 1,400 years of oppression against Christians will point to the various periods of Muslim tolerance regarding Christians, as the possible and desired alternative to the other periods of violence and persecution. One cannot deny that such periods of relative tolerance have existed. And yet all such periods of tolerance have been a one way [sic] experience, in which the Islamic rulers decide, according to their own judgment, whether the Christians and other non-Muslims are to be tolerated in their beliefs or not. It is never, and has never, ever, been a question of equality. Fundamentally, in the eyes of Islam, we Christians and all other non-Muslims are not equal, and are not to be treated as equal, only to be tolerated or not, depending upon the intensity of the spirit of Jihad that prevails at the time.

Such is the cycle of history that has recurred in the Middle East over the past 1,400 years, and with each successive cycle the number of Christians and other non-Muslims has decreased until we have reached the point which exists in Iraq today—the point of extinction. Argue as you will, but this coming extinction will likely soon be fact, and what then will anyone be able to say? That we were made extinct by natural disaster, or gentle migration? That the ISIS attacks were unprecedented? Or in our disappearance will the truth emerge—that we were persistently and steadily eliminated over the course of 1,400 years by a belief system which allowed for regular and recurring cycles of violence against us.

Not content to let the host country for his speech remain unscathed, Warda continued with a blistering assessment of Western ignorance concerning the reality of non-Muslims in the Middle East and failed US foreign policy in Iraq.

In these past years I have been blessed to spend a great deal of time in this country. I have spent time learning to understand your brave and never-ending commitment to equal rights for all citizens, and the power with which you utilize your freedom of speech. And I will tell you that were you to stand, truly stand, in the shoes of the Christians of Iraq, and those of many other countries of the Middle East, you would not accept for one day, one hour, one second, the status under which we live today—and under which we have lived for centuries. By our country's very Constitution, we are citizens of a lesser nature, deserving of tolerance from our self-appointed superiors, but at their discretion only and not in our own inherent right as equal children under a loving God.

So where, we ask, is there hope for the future in any of this? Should an ancient, peaceful people, be allowed to simply perish without comment, without objection? It seems an almost absurd question to ask in these modern times, does it not? Well then, we object. We object that one faith should have the right to kill another. We object. And we say that if there is to be any future for the Christians—and other religious minorities—of Iraq and the Middle East, there must be a change and a correction within Islam.

When asking whether ISIS is truly an "Islamic State" or an aberration and warping of Islamic theology, consider the following words, recently quoted in *Time* magazine:

"Western politicians should stop pretending that extremism and terrorism have nothing to do with Islam. There is a clear relationship between fundamentalism, terrorism, and the basic assumptions of Islamic orthodoxy. So long as we lack consensus regarding this matter, we cannot gain victory over fundamentalist violence within Islam."

and:

"The relationship between Muslims and non-Muslims, the relationship of Muslims with the state, and Muslims' relationship to the prevailing legal system wherever they live...Within the classical tradition, the relationship between Muslims and non-Muslims is assumed to be one of segregation and enmity. Perhaps there were reasons for this during the Middle Ages, when the tenets of Islamic orthodoxy were established, but in today's world such a doctrine is unreasonable. To the extent that Muslims adhere to this view of Islam, it renders them incapable of living harmoniously and peacefully within the multi-cultural, multi-religious societies of the 21st century."

Those words come not from some right wing political figure in the West, but from a leader of the largest Muslim organization in the world—Indonesian Islamic leader Yahya Cholil Staquf.[4]

---

4 Marco Stahlhut, "In Interview, Top Indonesian Muslim Scholar Says Stop Pretending That Orthodox Islam and Violence Aren't Linked," *Time*, September 8, 2017, accessed October, 2019, https://time.com/4930742/islam-terrorism-islamophobia-violence/

At present these sentiments may be more fully developed among Muslims in Asia than in the Middle East, but post-ISIS, we now hear similar things from Muslims in Iraq. Clearly, ISIS has shocked the conscience of the world, and has shocked the conscience of the Islamic majority world as well. The question now is whether or not Islam will continue on a political trajectory, in which Shari'a is the basis for civil law, and nearly every aspect of life is circumscribed by religion, or whether a more secular, tolerant movement will develop.

The West has not seen for some time anything like the totally religion-based theocratic systems in many Islamic majority countries. Why is it that the West finds it unremarkable that an organization exists called the Organization of Islamic Cooperation, with representation at the UN, etc. but there is no similar Organization of Christian Cooperation, or Organization of Buddhist Cooperation?

And what is it like to live under a system in which the faith upon which every law is based defines you as an infidel, or at best, a second, even third-class citizen? Too often, it has been for religious minorities in Iraq like it is with ISIS. And even when it is not, it has been always been a slow squeezing of our community. In fact, an academic study by my fellow Chaldean Bishop Bawai Soro shows that at no time since Iraq's conquest by Islam has the Christian percentage of the population grown. Some years it decreased slightly, other years more sharply, but the demographic trend for the past 1,400 years has always been unmistakably, relentlessly downward.

Secular observers in the West make two major mistakes in considering Islam. Either they consider it religious in the Christian (post-Papal State sense), which is to say somewhat removed from politics, or they view it through the lens of the mid-20th century, when more secular governments held sway in the Middle East, and in turn held political Islam at bay. But those largely secular governments (including those of Hussein, Qaddafi, Mubarak, etc.) are gone now. Now please do not misinterpret this to mean that these governments were without serious problems and deep injustice in their treatments of the people. But in their place now is something that is clearly worse—chaos and violence for all, and just beneath its surface flows the constant current of political Islam. And so now in the Mideast we have moved from fear, to terror, to horror. Where next?

One common misunderstanding that I wish to address with you in all this is the idea that the defeat of Daesh, or ISIS, means the defeat of this ideology of structured persecution and discrimination against non-Muslims. This is very far from the truth. In fact, while the physical fighting force of Daesh may have been defeated in a military sense, the idea of the re-establishment of the Caliphate has been firmly implanted in many minds throughout the Muslim world. And with this idea of the Caliphate there comes all the formal historical structures of intentional inequality and discrimination against non-Muslims.

I speak here not only of Iraq. We see leaders now in other countries in the Middle East who are clearly acting in a way which is consistent with the re-establishment of the Caliphate. How will you in the West react to this? My question to you is not rhetorical. The religious minorities of the Middle East want to know the answer. Will you continue to condone this never-ending structured persecution against us? When the next wave of violence begins to hit us, will anyone on your campuses hold demonstrations and carry signs that say, "we are all Christians," or "we are all Yazidis"?

And yes, I do say, the "next wave of violence," for this is simply the natural result of a ruling system that preaches inequality and justifies persecution. The math of this equation is not complicated. One group is taught that they are superior and legally entitled to treat others as inferior human beings on the sole basis of their faith and religious practices. This teaching inevitably leads to violence against any "inferiors" who refuse to change their faith. And there you have it—the history of Christians and religious minorities in the Middle East for the last 1,400 years.

Concerning political support, we ask that you support efforts by your leaders to ensure equal treatment for all minorities in Iraq. In this we pray that your policy makers can find in themselves the humility to recognize that their theories, which over the past decades have become our horrific reality, have been almost universally wrong, based in fundamentally flawed assessments of the Iraqi people and situation. And in these mistaken policies, designed in comfort and safety from afar, argued over in the media as partisan intellectual talking points, hundreds of thousands of innocent people have died. An entire country has been ripped apart and left to the jackals. This horror all began with policy, and we beg those of you who continue to have access in shaping policy for your country, the most powerful on earth, to daily remember that your policy assessments have life or death consequences. Please, walk humbly and make sure that you truly understand the people on whom you are passing sentence.

In the audience that day were former US government senior officials who had played a direct role in the US occupation of Iraq after 2003. Afterwards, one of them took me aside and said, "This speech is important. You need to make sure that it gets out."

CHAPTER 11

The Minority's Reality

"The problem," the driver said, "is that democracy cannot work here in Iraq."

We were in Baghdad in early 2017, and I sat in the back seat with the Chaldean priest, who looked at me knowingly and nodded his head. Outside, the traffic and chaos were endless in every direction, and we moved in fits while street vendors selling tea and sweets moved from car to car.

"You would want another Saddam?" I asked.

He lifted both hands off the steering wheel and held them up as if beseeching.

How many times in the last three years had I heard this? "Yes, Saddam was a tyrant but compared to what came after his was a Golden Time." It was a difficult proposition to take certainly if you were Kurdish or a Marsh Arab and the target of Saddam's genocide. But for many Muslims, it was mostly true, and for Christians, unquestionably so. In the run-up to the 2003 invasion of Iraq, the Christians had seen their doom in the offing and warned Washington, DC, to no avail. I thought of this conflict between Western views of what should be and the Middle Eastern views of their own realities many times. The issue was hardly unique to Iraq.

* * *

THE EGYPTIAN SAT ACROSS FROM ME, packed in amongst the people sitting under the stringed lights of the outside patio of the teahouse. Above us loomed the ancient presence of the Erbil Citadel. Around us the noise of the city swirled, and our conversation was audible only to the two of us. He was a member of the Coptic Orthodox Church and was visiting in Erbil for business. The twin bombings of churches on Palm Sunday in the Egyptian cities of Tanta and Alexandria had taken place just two days before, and as the updates on the news and the replays of the videos continued to roll on the television screens above us, his anguish showed.

"I was reading in the US media this morning about Islamophobia," he said. "The writer was talking about this," he gestured to the screen above, "and said that we needed to be aware of 'creeping Islamophobia.' He said that this attack was not the work of Islam and that to say it was so was Islamophobic."

He stirred his tea and worked his jaw.

"What people in your country. This," he waved at the screen, "is true Islam. To say this is so is Islamophobic? We are people who live under Islam. Your people do not know their own language."

He was a righteously angry man who spoke at least four very difficult languages fluently, plus English. I let him continue.

"What is a phobia? Do your people even know this? It is an irrational fear. Our fear of Islam is not irrational. We are not phobic about Islam. We are realistic. We live underneath it. Islam is trying to kill us. Our fear of it is completely rational."

He lit up a cigarette and inhaled deeply, holding it in for a long while before exhaling up into the cold night air.

With a Christian population still estimated at upwards of 10 million, from a number standpoint, the Christians of Egypt remained secure. But from every other measure, their persecution and exposure to violence was among the worst anywhere. Caught in the long and brutal struggle between often oppressive and authoritarian political regimes on the one hand, and Islamist opposition, often radical, on the other, the Christians, by the second decade of the twenty-first century, had become regular targets of terrorist attacks throughout the country. Bombings of churches, murders at gatherings, abductions, rapes, and violent intimidation occurred with numbing regularity. In February 2017, ISIS had called for the targeting of Christians, in part as a means of undermining the rule of President Fattah el-Sisi, who was waging a heavy fight against radical Islamist groups within the country. In the months that followed, terrorist attacks on Christians rose sharply, including the Palm Sunday bombings at St. George's in the city of Tanta and Saint Mark's in Alexandria.

"I will tell you something," he said, leaning closer. "This will not get better. This will get worse. Sisi cannot wipe these people out. There are too many of them. This will all continue, and the Christians will always be targets."

Later that month, he rented out his home in Cairo and moved his wife and three children out of the country.

* * *

It was late winter in 2018 in the town of Baghdede, and Fr. Thabet and I sat with the Syriac Catholic priest Fr. Georges and two of his fellow priests. Baghdede, also known as Qaraqosh, had been the largest Christian town in Nineveh before the ISIS war, with a Christian population nearing 50,000. The scene of heavy fighting during the war, much of Qaraqosh still lay in ruins. But thanks to the tireless work of Fr. Georges and his team, much of the city had slowly come back to life. Of the original Christian inhabitants, he estimated that as many as 26,000 had returned.

But the spirit of Fr. Georges and his brothers was low. Despite significant support from the private aid community and the nonstop efforts of his people, the spark of hope for their town was in danger. Of those that had returned, many had kept a foot back in Erbil where most had spent their years of displacement. Out in Nineveh, the Christians were facing an ongoing fight to maintain their place in the shifting power struggles in the region. Large scale infrastructure investments backed by USAID and the international community had improved basic access to power and water, but other projects were seemingly co-opted by Muslim or Shabak power factions as soon as they began. Already there was discussion within the Syriac Catholic community about establishing a formal separate Diocese in Erbil, an admission that for many of the Christians formerly of Baghdede, Erbil was their new home and where they saw their future.

Speaking with one of the priests, I asked what the mood was of the people.

"They are trying," he said. "But really, they have no choice. Most of these people here, they have no place left to go. But for the future, for their children, here in Baghdede they have very little hope."

"Look," he said, putting his finger on the table, "for many of these families their ancestors were first here from the north. They were persecuted and killed here by the Muslims, by the Kurds, so they moved to the south, to Baghdad and Basra. They lived there until they were persecuted and killed by the Muslims in the south, so then they moved north, many to Mosul, until they were persecuted and killed there by the Muslims, and then they moved here to Baghdede, where they were persecuted and killed by ISIS, so they moved to Erbil for two years, and now, there is no place else left in Iraq for them to go anymore. We have made the whole circle." With his finger, he drew a ring on the table.

I thought of Sabah, a teacher from Baghdede that had lived in the Sports center IDP camp that we had closed down two years earlier. He held a master's degree in English and had taught in Mosul and Baghdede before ISIS. During the displacement, he worked behind the counter in small restaurant across the street from the rectory. I would visit with him from time to time after his family had been moved out of the camp. When Baghdede was finally liberated, I asked if he would return.

"My friend," he said, smiling, "I just want to leave this fucking country."

"What about the programs that are coming to help people rebuild their homes?"

"People will take this money, they will fix their homes, and they will sell them and leave. If they can leave the country, this is what they will do. If they can't, they will come to Erbil until they can leave. The old people will stay, the people with government jobs will stay, and the people with businesses will stay. But for everybody else, I think they will leave as soon as they can. For me, as soon as I have some money to do it, I will leave."

* * *

ONE OF THE AREAS IN WHICH THE CHURCH had resettled the displaced Christians was the development of Ozal City several kilometers outside Erbil. Having managed to reach terms with the development's owners, the Church had already placed several hundred families there. Using temporary modular structures, a school and a church had been set up for the people, and a priest had been assigned to live there and tend to their needs. The school was run by the Jesuit fathers under the Jesuit Refugee Service, health care was available through the Slovakian clinic backed by the Knights of Columbus, and while the distance from Erbil proved to be a problem for some who were trying to get work, the community itself was a place of hope for the Christians there.

But when Deacon Shwan and I traveled out there to check on the status of the additional homes we wanted to rent, he took me aside before we returned.

"I must show you some people," he said. "They are Yazidis, and there is nobody to help them. We are giving them food from our program, and they can use the clinic. But they need some houses."

At the edge of the development, down a ravine next to giant storm drain, sat a cluster of huts: one made of salvaged cinder blocks and wood scraps, the others from remains of Quonset-style huts long ago discarded. UN logos showed on some tarp sections. Down the side of the ravine were heaps of garbage that had been tipped down over the years. Outside, two men sat listlessly under a makeshift awning while women in the striped dresses moved in and out of the dwellings. Shwan and I made our way down through the debris and walked over to the men.

They smiled when they saw Shwan. He had made friends with them some time ago and had continued to check on them over the months. They beckoned us to sit down with them, and a boy ran off inside one of the huts and came back out with two more plastic chairs.

"We will have some tea with them, and they can tell about their situation," said Shwan.

They had originally fled from outside of Mosul and ended up coming into Erbil with a group of Christians who they had fallen in with during the mass exodus from Nineveh. ISIS had been in their village before they were able to escape, and they had witnessed them taking away women and killing people in the street. When they reached Erbil, they were afraid to go into any of the UN camps because they believed there might be Muslims there. For these people, the breach with any trust of Islam had been complete, and they were deeply traumatized by what had happened and all they had seen.

With Shwan translating, the men told their story. At first, they had simply squatted in a vacant building in Erbil, but eventually they had been chased out. One of them had done day labor out in Ozal and knew there were some dumped materials outside the development and that there were Christians being moved out there. With that, the group of them, numbering around fifty, had moved out and put together the shelters.

"Has anybody helped you since you have been here?" I asked.

"Yes, the people from the Church," he answered, pointing up the hill.

"What about from the UN or anybody else, have they come see you here?"

"No, nobody."

"Did you go to speak with them?"

"No, we will not go to their camps. We have friends who are there. We will not go."

"But they will take care of you there."

"No, the Muslims run the camps for the UN, and we will not go there."

I looked over at Shwan. "You see," he said, "this is the situation. They are here, and they will not go. But they cannot live here in this situation. With this new money, can we help them?"

"Yes, I think so. We will see."

We finished our tea and thanked them, promising to return in the coming days. Arriving back in Erbil, I emailed to our contacts at the Nazarene Fund and requested permission to use a portion of the relocation funds for housing the Yazidis. They came back quickly asking for a day to work on it. They had raised funds for the purpose of helping the displaced Christians and needed to make sure the change in use of proceeds fit within the scope. I arranged to speak with them directly by phone and explained the totality of the situation and, within two hours, came the approval to proceed.

Three days later, Shwan and I drove back out to Ozal City on a blazing Friday morning. The elder of the Yazidi group invited us inside his home to shelter us all from the heat. His extended family was all inside a long Quonset-style hut, with plastic tarps run sideways to divide the space into multiple rooms. We sat in the front room on battered plastic chairs and wooden benches made from crate scraps. While the women quietly brought us out tea, Shwan explained the situation to them—the Church wanted to bring them out of these huts and provide them with group homes up on the streets above. The man gave a confused look and spoke rapidly to Shwan, smiling but not at all at ease.

"He is afraid we want to move him out from these homes and away from here."

Shwan spoke with him again, showing the singular patience and gentleness that he seemingly carried with him always. The elder asked many questions, then paused before asking many more, all the while Shwan answering in an even, soothing voice. Finally, he looked over to me.

"When we bring in the first new Christian families in these next days, I will show him also where we would like to move them. He wants to believe us that this is true. These are very poor people."

A week later, they were in their freshly-painted apartment, still using the box scrap furniture from their huts, but all smiles as they welcomed the two of us once again for tea. Now, for the first time, we began to see the whole family, including the girls and young women. A young man came out as well. He spoke working English and had hoped someday to go to university. Sitting there on the boxes with their thin covers of worn-out blankets and sheets, he told us their story.

When ISIS had first come into the village, they had arrived in one truck of five or six fighters. They told all the people to stay calm and that there was no need to run away. They were there now to protect them, and they would not be harmed. And with that, they drove off. Meanwhile, another group of Yazidis arrived several hours later and told them to run now. This is all a trick they said of the promise from the ISIS fighters. When they came back to our town, they shot dead all the men and took the women away. You must run now. They will come soon.

The terrified people had gathered what they could and began to flee the town, but the ISIS advance units were already entering the far end of the village. The people there had run into their homes, but the ISIS fighters were already dragging them out and forcing the men onto their knees before shooting them. As the women screamed in the streets, they were beaten and thrown in the backs of trucks. The Yazidis now in Ozal had only escaped because they were at the other end of the town, and there had not been enough ISIS fighters to control all the people they were killing and capturing where they had entered the town.

The Yazidis had crammed themselves into a small convoy of vehicles and, with lights turned off, had crept out of the town using a wide dirt path that met up the main road a mile further east. From there, they had driven without stopping to the first Kurdish checkpoint, where their car had been taken from them, and together with tens of thousands of other Yazidis, Christians, Shabak, and other Muslims, they began walking.

Along the way, they had come across an old Christian man, one of the many elderly orphans, who was sitting by the road next to wheelbarrow, weeping for help. He had been pushed that far by another Christian man, but this man and his wife had then been picked up by a family member who had managed to keep his car at the checkpoint. The old man had sent the young couple on their way, hoping that he could find the strength to walk for a while on his own, but his strength had failed him. The Yazidis had taken the old man into their group and took turns pushing him along.

"It was like this," the Yazidi said to me, looking down at the floor. "With the Christians, we are now like brothers. We can live with the Christians. But we will never live with the Muslims again, never."

"But they are not all ISIS, and many of them were killed too," I answered.

"The teaching is all the same," he answered. "Their teaching tells them they can kill us. It does not matter, Sunni, Shia. This one will kill us one day. The other will kill us the next. We can never trust any of them again."

I looked at his young, placid, even gentle face, but from his voice there was nothing but pure hatred. I asked him what he hoped for his future.

"I want to leave this country and study to be an engineer. But not here. I will go anyplace in the West or to Australia. But I will not stay here."

Later that same year, in December, we set about closing down one of the last of camps under the Nazarene project. In this one, several hundred families were living in an eight-story concrete skeleton of a structure, in which temporary panel walls had been fixed into place in order to make a crude apartment complex, with water provided in portable tanks and electricity pumped in from outside generators. Inside, families lived in one-room, container-like boxes, mostly ten by sixteen feet, with communal kitchen areas on each floor.

The residents of the building had formed their own small village of mixed Yazidi and Christian families. The Yazidis and the Christians there had all come from the same general area of Nineveh and had all occupied the apartment shell at the same time. In the ensuing two years, they had protected each other. Now, when it came time to finally move them out and into the rented group homes from the program, they each hesitated for the same reason—when Shwan approached the Christians about preparing to leave, one of their first concerns had been what would happen to their Yazidi neighbors. And when Shwan then spoke with the Yazidi elders, they asked much the same question—where will our Christian neighbors go? In the end, they were all moved out at the same time, but I could not help but wonder whether the commonality of their experience would ever forge something lasting.

CHAPTER 12

Failing While the Window Closes

A brief opportunity to formally cement a substantive, working Chris-
tian-Yazidi partnership occurred in the opening of the USAID Broad
Agency Announcement (BAA) that followed in the wake of Vice President Pence's aid policy statement in October of 2017. Following upon
what both the Yazidi and Christian community in Iraq understood to
be a promise by the US to provide direct funding and support into the
indigenous minority-run programs, the Yazidi and Christian leaders
joined together as partners to submit two substantive proposals to
USAID. The first was for the establishment of an Institute for Cultural
Preservation, the second, to fund a center for Property Rights. Both
proposals fit squarely within long-established USAID paradigms for
successful restoration and rehabilitation of conflict-affected areas. By
having structured the proposals as formal partnerships involving the
two minority groups which had been found by the US to have been
victims of genocide, the Christians and Yazidis had heavy hopes that
real support would be coming from the US to back up the promises of
the vice president.

At the concept stage, both proposals were given a green light to
proceed, and as the decision-making process moved into the spring of
2018, the Christians and Yazidis waited in anticipation of formal award

announcements. But in what can only be viewed as a fiasco of management, the entire BAA process was subverted and redirected within USAID in the awarding process. In April of 2018, as the email announcements began to circulate in the aid community, the Christians and Yazidis found that both of the projects they had submitted in partnership had been rejected. The rejection came in the form of a summary email, which provided no detail or reasoning beyond stating that there was no appeal and that USAID was under no legal requirement to provide further information for their decision. Seeking clarification nonetheless, I emailed back to the address of the sender within USAID only to receive an auto reply that the sender was on leave for the next three weeks.

Slowly, as the various applicants began comparing rejection letters, it became clear that no proposals from groups based in Iraq, including the local faith-based groups which the vice president had referred to in the promises of his speech, had been approved. Instead, the only groups to have received approval notices were three large, US-based professional aid organizations, all of them well-established within the existing USAID/UN funding pipeline. None of them had been deeply engaged, if at all, in assisting the displaced Christians over the prior three years. Most shocking of all, the largest recipient of funding was to be a project led by IOM, the International Organization of Migrants, which was formally related to the UN and one of the UN's major implementing arms. This went against the public statements of Vice President Pence that the US would "stop funding ineffective relief efforts at the United Nations and from this day forward, America will provide support directly to persecuted communities through USAID."

Clearly, the promises of the vice president had been undercut, whether intentionally or through the sheer weight and inertia of the established aid funding system. Had those in charge of implementing the BAA intentionally sought to undermine the vice president, or had they simply taken the easy decision and funded projects to entities they already knew well? For the Christians and the Yazidis, the effect was the same. Just as with the genocide declaration, they had been promised help, and it had not come.

By coincidence, Archbishop Warda and I were in Washington, DC, at the time the rejection notices were sent out. In what we had planned to be a positive foundational visit which would hopefully build upon the anticipated awards from USAID, we had scheduled meetings with numerous government and academic leaders. Although we were not certain that our projects would be fully approved, at minimum we understood that USAID would look to partner us with more experienced USAID recipients, so that our projects could at least move forward with our input and participation. But as the reality of what had taken place in the BAA awarding process became clear, a feeling of utter frustration and disappointment spread through our entire community of support- ers both in the US and around the world. In angry closed-door meetings and private phone calls, the management of USAID was excoriated by concerned members of Congress and highly-placed supporters of the persecuted minorities in Iraq.

Media coverage was harsh as well, culminating in a brutally frank editorial that ran in *The Wall Street Journal*. Authored by Congressman Chris Smith (R) of New Jersey and former Reagan National Security Advisor Bud McFarlane, the opinion piece, published on June 7, 2018, was titled, "Iraqi Christians Are Still Waiting, Mr. Pence—In October he said help would be on the way. So where is it?" Citing directly from the vice president's October speech, the editorial read:

"While faith-based groups with proven track records and deep roots in these communities are more than willing to assist, the United Nations too often denies their funding requests," Mr. Pence said last year. "My friends those days are over."

Except those days aren't over. Career staff at USAID have ignored Mr. Pence's words and thwarted the clear intent of the Trump adminis- tration. As a result, the light of Iraqi Christianity could be permanently extinguished."[1]

Understandably stung by the public criticism, Pence's office announced an immediate visit to Iraq by the USAID administrator, Mark Green to address the situation. In announcing the visit, the

---

[1] Robert McFarlane and Chris Smith, "Iraqi Christians Are Still Waiting, Mr. Pence," *The Wall Street Journal*, June 7, 2018, accessed October, 2019, https://www.wsj.com/articles/iraqi-christians-are-still-waiting-mr-pence-1528413035.

statement from the vice president's office read, "President Trump and Vice President Pence made restoring the rights and property of Iraq's Christian and Yazidi communities a top, and unceasing, priority. The Vice President will not tolerate bureaucratic delays in implementing the administration's vision to deliver the assistance we promised to the people we pledged to help."[2] In a statement issued by Green concerning his pending visit, he promised to develop "a plan of action to accelerate aid to those in greatest need."[3] Green's delegation would come and go in July, and a shakeup of mid-level staff at the USAID Mission would take place that summer. A special envoy from the vice president, Max Primorac, would be stationed in Erbil in August 2018, and he would spend the next year in an uphill and often single-handed effort to change the course of aid implementation in Nineveh in general accordance with the promises of the vice president. But for the foundational projects put forward by the local Christian organizations which had been the focus of the help promised by the vice president in 2017, nothing would change. By August 2019, the once critical programs envisioned by the Archdiocese of Erbil and its partners under the BAA were largely moot—still unfunded, overrun by time, circumstance, and the power factions that had pushed themselves into the empty spaces, spaces that, for over a thousand years, had been home to some of the world's oldest Christians.

But in retrospect, despite all our efforts to preserve a viable Christian presence in Nineveh, by the summer of 2018, we already knew that our ship of hope had been hulled. Every month had been as a year to our cause, and now there we were, a year and half since the liberation of Nineveh, with the restoration and return of the Christians growing less plausible day by day. We had spent years of critical human and financial resources trying to bring help and positive change while there was still time, and everywhere, we were being undermined, misled, or outmaneuvered. Most distressing was the growing realization that our fight for survival was increasingly being hit as collateral damage, seemingly

---

[2] "Statement from the Office of the Vice President," The Whitehouse, June 8, 2018, accessed October, 2019, https://www.whitehouse.gov/briefings-statements/statement-office-vice-president-2.

[3] "Statement by USAID Administrator Mark Green," USAID, June 8, 2018, accessed October, 2019, https://www.usaid.gov/news-information/press-releases/jun-8-2018-statement-usaid-administrator-mark-green.

without concern, from the nonstop barrage aimed at the Trump administration by its opponents. Sitting in a private breakfast in Washington, DC, before returning to Iraq, I looked around the table at the small group of advocates and government people who had been our supporters from the very outset of the crisis in 2014.

"Before we all leave," I said, "there is something I want to say to you all. You deserve to know the truth, and you need to know it as well. We are out of time, and anything that comes now is likely too late. Our window has closed for keeping most of these towns. I am not saying we should give up. Things could still change, and there is no telling what might happen to the seeds we might still plant, so there is always hope. But realistically, we need to start thinking about the Christians of Iraq as a remnant people, and Nineveh as mostly finished for them."

They all knew it, and I felt terrible for having to say it. They had given years of their lives to this effort and believed in it. Would any of it turn out to have mattered? It weighed on all of us like the end.

CHAPTER 13

Lessons and Truths

In drawing lessons from the vanishing presence of the Christians of Iraq, the contributing factors are myriad, changing in specific importance and impact over the last 1,400 years in which they have traveled the long road to disappearance. But in what has transpired over the last two decades, specific lessons can be clearly identified which require honest recognition, if not for the Christians of Iraq themselves, at least for what their tragedy warns for the rest of humanity, if it is willing to listen. Nowhere is the willingness to listen to the reality of this tragedy more important than in the West, particularly the US, whose presence, for better or worse, still dominates so much of the world and whose footprint is now indelibly left in the debris and chaos of twenty-first century Iraq.

A starting point for any honest assessment from the US is the unavoidable recognition that those decision makers behind the Iraq invasion of 2003 have blood on their hands, and history will not let it be washed away. The myth of Saddam's weapons of mass destruction having long since been disproven, the moral responsibility for the decision to invade Iraq falls squarely on those in the US, led by the Bush administration, who drove this disastrous folly. Nowhere does this moral responsibility lie more deeply than the utter incompetence and lack of understanding shown in the planning for the aftermath of Saddam's overthrow. The decision to disband the Iraqi army and create a vacuum for the country's internal security deserves further historical analysis and scrutiny of the most detailed nature possible. In the wake of the years of unending civil terror and blood that followed this decision, history still does not know how many people have been killed or displaced. In deaths, the numbers vary from hundreds of thousands to as much as one million. In displaced and refugees, the numbers are well into the millions. Indeed, with the continuing presence of ISIS and the unrelenting civil strife between Shia, Sunni, and Kurd, these numbers continue to grow. All of this has, as its most identifiable immediate proximate cause, the underlying decisions made by the US in their invasion and occupation of Iraq.

As Archbishop Warda stated in his Georgetown speech, "This horror all began with policy," and these "policy assessments have life or death consequences," the consequences of which demand that those making such assessments, "walk humbly and make sure that you truly understand the people on whom you are passing sentence."[1]

Implicit in the words of the archbishop are not simply that you must be absolutely and morally certain that you fully understand the justifications and consequences of invading another country, but once having done so, you are then barred from simply choosing the expedient course of action in extricating yourself from the mortal chaos which you have created.[2]

One such expedient action, from which the Christians and other minorities of Iraq will continue to suffer for decades to come, is the present Iraqi constitution itself, approved in 2005 while the US was still fully in control of ultimate decision-making in the country. Having expended a tragic and astounding amount of blood and treasure in taking over Iraq, the US overseers of the country then balked at the serious decisions necessary to bring the country fully into the world of modern democratic nations. This is reflected most clearly in Article Two of the Iraqi Constitution which declares:

---

1 Warda, "The Future of Religious Pluralism in Iraq."

2 In the months ahead of the US Invasion of Iraq in 2003, the Vatican under Pope John Paul II waged a desperate argument with US President George W. Bush to refrain from war, with a prophetic warning that it would be a "disaster" and that "you might start, and you don't know how to end it." https://edition.cnn.com/2003/ALLPOLITICS/03/05/sprj.irq.bush.vatican/

Islam is the official religion of the State and is a foundation source of legislation:

A. No law may be enacted that contradicts the established provisions of Islam.[3]

And what of the fundamental American and Western principle of separation of church and state? What of the "established provisions of Islam" that relegate all non-Muslims to second class or *dhimmi* status? How was it that the American decision makers and planners decided that this was an issue on which to concede, to be expedient? How was it not understood that, in formally constituting the continuance of this state domination of one faith over all others, they had effectively laid the groundwork for permanent, state-sanctioned discrimination and persecution? Protestations have been made that later listed articles of the Iraqi Constitution provide sufficient protections for minorities, but in the reality of Iraq today, these protestations have been borne out as Western legal sophistry. Under the constitution approved by the US, Islam would firmly rule Iraq. Non-Muslims would clearly and objectively be second-class citizens. Who conducted the analysis, and who made the decisions in the US, ultimately, to be complicit with the apparent expediency of this decision, for which the Christians and Yazidis continue to pay the fullest price? Or, from another, perhaps even more disturbing perspective, was the constitutionally-enshrined discrimination of religious minorities an aspect of the US planning for post-invasion Iraq that had already been fully considered and simply put aside as being of collateral importance? Of critical importance here is an honest acceptance of the fact that the US under the Bush administration did not seek simply to neutralize the behavior of Saddam Hussein. The US invaded and took possession of an entire country with the intention to rebuild it as a responsible member of the international community. Then, in a test of enormous fundamental importance—whether or not Iraq would be a country that supports, in law, the establishment of religious freedom—the US utterly, historically, failed.

---

[3] Iraq Constitution of 2005, accessed October 2019, https://www.constituteproject.org/constitution/Iraq_2005.pdf?lang=en.

A second example of expediency can be found in the contortion of public statements used by the US to characterize the Iraqi government as being a functioning state with a foundational democracy at the time of the US withdrawal under the Obama administration. While the continued deployment of US troops presented enormous complexities and no easy options, President Obama's 2011 description of Iraq as "sovereign, self-reliant, and democratic" is either a failed intelligence assessment of tragically epic proportions or an act of almost brazen public deception, justified only by political expediency. The rise of ISIS was not unforeseeable for anybody in Iraq. During the first two years of the Obama administration, the Christian leaders implored Americans, both in public and in private, not to be precipitous in leaving the country, knowing that, in the vacuum of security control, it would be the minorities who suffered first. The disintegration of security and protection for minorities in Baghdad and elsewhere that had already taken place post 2003 had taught the Christians that all too clearly.

In the decision to leave Iraq, in particular northern Iraq, using the public justification that the country was now sovereign, under control, and stabilized, was the likely impact on the minority Christians and Yazidis ever analyzed? And again, if so, was the outcome of this analysis either an astounding failure of intelligence, or was accurate intelligence provided and ultimately discarded as inconvenient to the preferred public narrative, with the fate of the minorities factored in as collaterally acceptable?

Somewhere in the midst of this murk for both of these examples, there are American officials and analysts who made calculated decisions using rationales that are far more complex and considered than what the public story has to date disclosed. Hundreds of thousands of innocent minorities in Iraq, have suffered, and continue to suffer, as a result.

Looming over all of this is the overwhelming specter of the dead, wounded, and traumatized on all sides. For the US, the number of those killed in action in Iraq since 2003 is over 4,400 and still counting, with the number of those wounded in action over 32,000, many of them permanently maimed and disabled.[4] For the Iraqis, including civilians, the

---

[4] US Department of Defense, Casualty Status Report, as of Oct. 28, 2019, accessed October, 2019, https://www.defense.gov/casualty.pdf.

numbers range from the low hundred-thousands to nearly one million killed, with an equal or greater number of wounded.[5]

For any Americans with ties to the military community, they know that these are just base numbers, with the total impact to families and loved ones exponentially greater. For every soldier that never came home, there were casualties still in the US whose lives were shattered as well. For every soldier that came home permanently disabled, there was a career that was ended and a family that was thrown into turmoil. And for many, the continued strain of multiple deployments ultimately destroyed the family relationships that had been put on hold. For many of those that managed to return unscathed physically, the horror of war that they had experienced stayed with them in the form of trauma leading to drug and alcohol abuse, and often worse. Suicide among active duty and returning veterans is an ongoing and open national disgrace and tragedy.

For every American soldier and family affected, the number is multiplied three- and fourfold for the people of Iraq. An entire generation has been physically and emotionally traumatized by war, and the lasting damage pervades the entire society. This is especially so amongst the male population living in a culture in which weakness cannot be shown. As such, proper care and counseling is most often ignored even in the rare occasions in which it is made available to the public. We need only to examine the depressing statistics of Vietnam era vets in the US to understand the long-term implications of this suppressed trauma and experience. While openness to counseling shows greater potential among women and children for some limited effectiveness in Iraq, access to such help remains greatly limited. In nearly all cases, it is relegated to a lower priority than income and security. The impact of long-term scarring to the children will prove itself out in the coming decades.

As for lessons to be drawn from the US policy of the last several years, particularly as it affects the persecuted minorities, the clearest takeaway is that stated intention is not enough. Mere words without thorough follow-through can make even the statements themselves,

---

[5] Philip Bump, "15 Years after the Iraq War began, the death toll is still murky," *Washington Post*, March 20, 2018, accessed October, 2019, https://www.washingtonpost.com/news/politics/wp/2018/03/20/15-years-after-it-began-the-death-toll-from-the-iraq-war-is-still-murky.

no matter how well intended, a source of increased harm and exposure to those the statements were originally intended to help. In Iraq, this played out clearly in two instances—first in the declaration of genocide, and second in the announcement in October of 2017 that the US would begin directly funding the working organizations on the ground in Iraq rather than working exclusively through the UN.

In the case of the genocide declaration by Secretary Kerry under the Obama administration, after an initial hope that support and recognition would now come to address the plight of the affected minorities, it became clear that in the US there was no follow-up plan, no new directive that would take place. Instead, the initial hope that came with the declaration drifted away, such that by the time the Trump administration took over, there was a growing concern that the incoming secretary of state, Rex Tillerson, had no intention to pursue it further. Perhaps he was even taking quiet steps to back away from it. A forceful barrage of editorials and warnings from the tireless advocates for the affected minorities eventually resulted in clear public affirmation of the genocide declaration by Tillerson, but in Iraq, still, nothing else changed.

On the ground in Iraq, the genocide declaration effort had consumed a tremendous amount of assets, both human and financial, from the displaced and affected communities. Dwindling energy and scarce resources which otherwise might have been spent on more immediate needs were put aside by the displaced communities in the mistaken belief that the genocide declaration itself would result in an immediate flow of increased aid and protection. In the raising of expectations by those who worked on the genocide effort in Iraq, there is perhaps a cautionary tale as well.

Matters only grew further confused as the formal designation of genocide status continued to play out differently in the EU and the UN. Believing that the designation from the US secretary of state would drive the remainder of the Western governments and the UN to follow suit, the Christians instead found themselves as the subject of what were increasingly political arguments in the West. By 2018, the view of the Iraqi Christians towards the genocide declaration was that while deeply welcome from a standpoint of moral support, it would not be resulting in any material change on the ground. While the work of the small group of relentless core supporters of the declaration presents a heroic story in its own right, the grudging acceptance by the US State Department, in which they had been publicly forced into agreement, appeared to carry with it a built-in reluctance for meaningful follow-through. In all of this, the Iraq genocide designation effort and its impact presents a worthy case study for further review for the benefit of future genocide questions.

The genocide declaration may yet prove to be of greater lasting value over time. Substantial issues regarding property rights and reparations have yet to even begin playing out. The ultimate destination of the displaced Christians in the diaspora remains an open question as well. Additionally, the genocide declaration unquestionably served as the key support for the enactment of H.R. 390, the Iraq and Syria Genocide Relief Act—a law which may prove of significant benefit to the affected people in the coming years. In all these cases, the genocide determination may prove pivotal. In any case, the effort to fight for the designation stands on its own for the decency and human compassion that drove it.

A second critical example in which well-placed intention was undermined by lack of follow-through came in the form of the apparent fundamental policy shift announced by Vice President Pence in October of 2017. Of primary importance in this instance was the lack of any written presidential directive or executive order to provide working teeth to the policy announcement. Issuing such an order or directive was generally standard following any major policy announcement. In such cases, the issuance and forwarding of the directive to the involved government offices and missions provided both clarity and a means of ensuring compliance with the stated objectives of the policy decision.

For the Trump administration, this omission created difficulties at several levels. First, in the hostile environment of established Washington, DC, that followed the Trump election, many career officials were simply opposed to anything coming from the administration. Second, it created difficulties within the State Department and USAID. Deep and long-term working connections existed between USAID and the UN, with many careers involving time spent moving between the two organizations. The public humiliation of the UN contained in the vice president's speech had angered many still in positions of authority within the State Department and USAID. Within the UN, to the public rebuke was added the even more concerning reality that they were soon to potentially see a significant loss of funding. Not surprisingly, many of those at USAID, the State Department, and the UN fought back through the most effective means at their disposal—the slowdown. In this, they had been given an invaluable means of cover through the non-existence of a written order or directive. When pressed on matters related to the implementation of the new policy, they could simply respond that they had received no written directive on the matter and were therefore proceeding as usual.

Again, the failure of the administration to issue the order or directive remains curious. The fact that it was being used as a regular cover for non-compliance with the administration's public statements was no secret within the State Department. Sympathetic government staff regularly lamented the issue in their conversations with us.

The uncertainty surrounding the coverage of the newly-stated policy also worked against the Christians in another way. While the full context of the vice president's speech had clearly indicated a desire to make sure that a viable Christian community remained in Iraq, his specific language was largely restricted to the return of the displaced Christians to the Nineveh Plain. While this was certainly one of the primary concerns at the time for the Christians, in terms of ensuring a continuing Christian presence in Iraq, Nineveh was far from the only concern.

The ISIS war, and the decade preceding it, had created a group of permanently displaced Christians who had settled throughout Iraq, many of them in Erbil, but some in Baghdad and elsewhere. In Nineveh province, many people whose homes had been completely destroyed had no meaningful assistance programs available to rebuild from the ground up. From Mosul and Telkayf, moreover, the displaced Christians had no intention of ever returning due to the deep current of ISIS sympathy that had encouraged their lifelong neighbors to turn against them and call them out publicly, painting identifying initials and symbols on their doors as ISIS came to take control. The most obvious modern comparison can only be that of the Jews in Germany during the rise of the Nazis. To ask the Christians to return to Mosul would have been the equivalent of asking the Jews to return to Berlin after World War II.

As a consequence, many Iraqi Christians formerly from Nineveh Province had already begun committing themselves to rebuilding their lives in Erbil and elsewhere. But just as with the other displaced Christians, they had nearly all been robbed of everything and had nothing from which to rebuild their lives. As the only meaningful help that they had received throughout the displacement came from the Church, they understandably turned in that direction when they learned that funds were to be provided from the US to help the displaced Christians of Iraq. Throughout the winter of 2017 and into the summer of 2018 and beyond, the Archdiocese of Erbil and others within the Church in Iraq made repeated requests to the US for assistance in helping with these permanently displaced people.

Moreover, throughout 2018, a new influx of Christian refugees began to appear in Erbil—Christians from the country of Syria escaping the violence there and moving to a third country in order to gain refugee status with the UNHCR. While their presence in Erbil was technically transitory, in the global morass of conflicting immigration policies, the likely stay of most of these families would be years. As word had passed throughout the Christian communities of the Middle East that Christians could live openly and in general safety in the enclave of Ankawa in Erbil, new Syrian families arrived daily into the community. While the archdiocese did its best to provide help to these families, it soon grew beyond the capability of the Church to manage on its own.

But throughout this time, when the Church would make proposals, the response would be that the present efforts were limited to Nineveh, as stated in the vice president's speech, and there was no other written directive which would allow for stabilization funding to go to areas outside Nineveh, despite the fact that substantial numbers of permanently displaced Christian refugees remained in desperate need in these other areas. For the Church and the Christian leaders, it was incomprehensible that the government of the US could not either see the need or find a way to support the displaced Christians outside Nineveh.

The matter came to a head in the early spring of 2019, when after months of speeches and public statements from the administration and USAID—that they were committing hundreds of millions of dollars to areas affecting the displaced Christians—the permanently displaced

Christians from Mosul themselves began to angrily protest to the Archdiocese of Erbil that they were being ignored. Misunderstanding the nuanced language of the American speeches, the Iraqi Christians had assumed that the Archdiocese of Erbil itself had been the recipient of funding and was directing it all to Nineveh or other projects, and not making any accommodation for the permanently displaced families still under its care in Erbil. In fact, at the time, the Archdiocese of Erbil had still yet to receive any direct funding whatsoever from the US and had seen the majority of its private donor support drop away in the mistaken belief by the donors—as had been the case with the displaced families—that the US government was now providing substantial direct assistance to the archdiocese.

The confusion was compounded by a similar misunderstanding in the international media, which had latched on to the same speeches by the administration and USAID that seemed to indicate that substantial funding was going directly to the archdiocese and other church groups. Caught in a no-win position, the archdiocese sought to clarify the truth of the funding situation—in which it was still outside desperately looking in—and, at the same time, not disparage the efforts of the vice president, which the archdiocese believed to be genuine, and for which they were deeply grateful. The resulting confusion strained relationships on all sides, and once again, scarce human and financial resources were spent in addressing small but constant crises of confidence and partnership that should never have occurred in the first place. A clear, written executive order or presidential directive in the days following the vice president's speech might not have avoided all of these issues, but it would have prepared a vastly different landscape than the thorny hedgerows of confusion that ensued.

A further area of tremendous importance is the apparent lack of appreciation by American diplomats and policy makers as to the lasting impact of the radical shifts in commitment and presence that are present from one presidential administration to the next. While the deference to power that is given to the Americans whenever they are actively engaged is beyond question, so too is the realization, especially in Iraq, that US policy is always driven by politics at home and therefore changeable from one administration to the next and even one election cycle to the next. The result is that while respect is afforded to the administration in power, the players in Iraq and the Middle East all know that the American government is often an unreliable partner. For many countries in the region, they felt they had often paid a dear price for ending up on the wrong side of that partnership when the domestic currents in the US had changed. As a result, especially in Iraq, the US word of commitment over the past two decades has become a devalued coin, perhaps to a degree far greater than US pride is often willing to admit.

This inducement to hedging when dealing with the US played itself out with frustrating clarity in the continuing influence of the Iranian backed *Hashd Al Shaabi* units in Iraq. While the US continued to apply what it believed would be a winning strategy of direct pressure on the Iraqi government to make a clear choice between Washington, DC, and Teheran, the myriad of competing interests in Iraq managed to continually stall, shift, and pose. All the while, the *Hashd* units and their Iranian backed politicians were able to bide their time and take their wins as the opportunities presented. For the Christians, this has had a nearly fatal effect on the return to the towns still under the control of the *Hashd*. Convinced by American diplomats to withhold attempting to return to their towns while the *Hashd* units remained, on the promise that the *Hashd* units would soon be removed ahead of massive US investment, the Christians instead saw months, then seasons, roll by with the *Hashd* still in power. Often, the *Hashd* were in open defiance of a central government in Baghdad which continually appeared either unwilling, or powerless, to force any change. The mostly unspoken hard truth underlying it all was that, for many of those in power in Baghdad at the time, the Iranians were seen as the better, more reliable ally.

For the displaced Christians, the continued entrenchment of the 30th and 50th *Hashd* Brigades in northern Nineveh throughout the summer of 2019 had sapped their trust in everybody. This increasingly included the leaders of their churches, many of whom had publicly supported the removal of the *Hashd*, believing, or perhaps hoping, that the Americans were actually going to succeed. Speaking with one of the priests in northern Nineveh in July of 2019, he said with great frustration, "the people do not trust anybody anymore. Not the government, not the US, not even the Church. We have all told them to wait and that these *Hashd* will be gone, but all they see is that these *Hashd* are still there. Most of these people, now, I think they will leave Iraq."

This issue of reliability is hardly unique to the Trump administration but is, rather, endemic in the continually changing priorities inherent in our politically-driven foreign policy process. As one priest from Baghdad told me in 2016, "You Americans are all over. Who can trust you? George Bush, he was a feared man with a big ego, but that made people want to fight him. And then what did he do? Disaster, he made a disaster. Then he is gone. Obama, nobody fears him. They call him *Sheikh, Sheikh Obama*, and they know that he will do nothing."

In dealing with the US, recent history has taught the Iraqis that, militarily, the US are the confident destroyers, capable of wiping out anything at anytime once they choose to do so. The power and reach of the US military is feared by the average Iraqi to a degree that would astonish most Americans. But the last several decades have also taught the Iraqis that behind the all-powerful US military, arrives the US government, and its record is far less certain. Iraqis have learned to understand the career-preservation and advancement climate that permeates much of the US government, and that if they are able to wait long enough, the person they are dealing with will change, along with all the rules and promises. Demanding that the Iraqis make bold choices to break from close working relations with pariah neighbor states might be the morally right path for the US to take, but pegging it on a promise of a consistent long-term US commitment is putting a heavy load on a slim branch.

* * *

IN EXAMINING THE IMPACT OF ISLAM AND ISLAMOPHOBIA on the status of the Christians of Iraq and the Middle East, we come to a point where hard truths must be faced. The first of these is the falseness of the proposition that somehow a zero-sum equation exists in which help for the Christians must always equate to discrimination against the Muslims. Perhaps no other argument was more frequently thrown against our efforts than this.

Christian townspeople in native dress prepare for a Palm Sunday procession in April, 2017 in Teleskof, Nineveh Plain, Northern Iraq. Teleskof was the first Christian town of Nineveh to recover from ISIS due in large part to an innovative and timely grant from the government of Hungary through its "Hungary Helps" program.

In 2017, I stood in the European Parliament and spoke to an assembly as part of a panel of witnesses regarding the restoration and stabilization of Iraq after ISIS. In going through our different projects to date, I listed the singular success of the support from the government of Hungary in the rapid rebuild of the town of Teleskof. While not wanting to wade into the internal disagreements between Hungary and other EU member states, I held up the Hungarian support as a cost-effective model which actually worked in a timely fashion and which properly addressed the urgency at hand. In doing so, I challenged other EU members far wealthier than Hungary as to why they could not act in an equally effective manner, noting that, from most of them, we had received no help since the outset of the crisis. Immediately came the objection that the Hungary program and our efforts were a form of discrimination against the Muslims who had suffered equally during the war. I had heard it many times before, and I posed a question back.

"Soon you will all be engaged in discussions regarding the return and rebuilding of Mosul. It is right that you should do so. The people there will need your help. But with the first Euro you spend on Mosul, you should understand that you are discriminating against the Christians who do not live there anymore, the Christians who were forced out under threats of violence by their own neighbors and whose persecution you will complete when you help to rebuild a city from which the Christians have been cleansed. And for these homeless Christians of Mosul, they do not exist anywhere in the plans of the EU or the UN. So please tell me, who is discriminating here?"

Many innocent Muslims suffered as a result of the ISIS war. They need help. But the help they need is in substantive ways different from the help needed for the Christians, if we accept that the continued existence of the Christians is any kind of priority for Iraq, and the world at large. The Muslim population of Iraq is not on the verge of disappearing. The Christian population of Iraq may disappear within the next decade. They both need help, and every temporary focus on one should not be shouted down as discriminatory against the other. Educated Western leaders who submit to this line of thinking, that help for the Christians automatically raises concerns of discrimination against Muslims, are in a very real way allowing themselves to become complicit in the end of Christianity in Iraq.

In addressing, even briefly, the issue of Islamophobia, we must start with the central admission that it exists, and where it does, it should be confronted. But where it does not exist, it should not be allowed as a blanket response to every real question about the treatment of minorities in countries under Islamic rule. For the Christians of Iraq and the Middle East, perhaps no other issue raises greater anguish than the perception in the West that the eastern Christians are not subjected to mistreatment under Islam, and that the acts of ISIS were not related in any way to Islamic teaching.

On a visit to the US in 2017, Fr. Douglas Bazi, the Chaldean priest from Baghdad had this to say about the nature of ISIS, "I ask about this word Daesh (the accepted derogatory slang for ISIS). Should we not call them the Islamic State, as they want to be called? For they claim that they are practicing pure Islam, and it is clear that many Muslims believe this. Muslims throughout the world should admit this and answer how this can be? The West should admit this. I do not say that all Muslims are bad, and for sure, many Muslims have been victims of ISIS as well, but this action of ISIS, they claim this is pure Islam, and clearly many Muslims believe they are right to call it so, and we should not be afraid to talk about it."

In 2014, the then Chaldean archbishop of Mosul, Emil Nona, speaking out in agony with this warning for the West after he lost his entire diocese overnight to ISIS with the willing assistance of much of the Muslim population of Mosul who had been neighbors to the Christian minority for centuries, "Your liberal and democratic principles are worth nothing here. You must consider again our reality in the Middle East, because you are welcoming in your countries an ever-growing number of Muslims. You think all men are equal, but Islam does not say that all men are equal. Your values are not their values."[6] If supporters in the West and elsewhere of a moderate Islam, which is able to co-exist in the modern world, are truly intent on countering the views of the minorities living under Islam, they will need to begin by a fundamental acceptance of the historical and continuing reality of a violent Islam that remains the common experience of the Christians and minorities in the Middle East.

In this analysis, it is critical to understand that the advent of ISIS is not an isolated event in the minds of the Christians. I recall a conversation with Fr. Emmanuel of the Ashti Camp in the spring of 2016.

"Don't think," he said, "that all this began with ISIS in 2014. No." He raised one hand and waved his index finger back and forth. "I am from

---

6 "Archbishop of Mosul: "Your liberal and democratic principles are worth nothing here," archbishopcranmer.com, August 19, 2014, accessed October, 2019, https://archbishopcranmer.com/archbishop-of-mosul-your-liberal-and-democratic-principles-are-worth-nothing-here.

Mosul, and I will tell you what happened there. In 2003, after the US invasion, there were announcements broadcast from the speakers on the Mosques, and they told the Muslims of Mosul, 'Don't buy houses from the Christians, soon we will take them for nothing.' So you see, the situation was clear even then, so don't think that this way of thinking just began in 2014 with ISIS."

One of the fears that was regularly raised amongst Iraqi Christians in the discussions regarding war crimes trials, as part of the genocide declaration, was that the international community would leave the cases with the local authorities in Iraq. Insisting on trials in a legitimate international forum would require the perpetrators to admit their guilt to the world or defend their proposition—that they were acting in true adherence to their faith. For the Christians, it galled them that, in all of the Islamic world, there had been no apologies for what had been done to the innocents in Iraq under marauders claiming the flag of Islam. All the while, there had been unending denials from throughout Islam that this did not represent the true faith. For the Christians of Iraq, they wanted Islam to have to confront this in the open, before the eyes of the whole world. The Iraqi Christians saw this as the only way in which there might be some form of acceptance of guilt, of responsibility for what the Christians believed so much of Islam had become. Without this public acceptance of responsibility in front of the global community, the Christians believed that the entire effort at justice would just be viewed by the perpetrators as the victors choosing who dies. For the Christians this provided no base from which talks of reconciliation could even begin. Meanwhile, the fundamental issue of underlying teachings and ideology would be left to smolder until its next outbreak of murder against innocents.

Islamophobia exists, and it should be confronted. But in Iraq and Syria, thousands of believers flying a flag, which they claimed to be of Islam, murdered and raped thousands of innocent non-Muslims, while thousands of other Muslims waved the same flag and cheered them on. To say this happened and demand lasting justice and accountability for it, including an honest public reckoning of the teaching and ideology behind it, is not Islamophobic. No legitimate nation or people should tolerate that as a response to what took place.

* * *

IN THE SPRING OF 2019, USAID began consideration of a proposal to provide assistance to the thousands of displaced families still remaining in the greater Erbil region. The program would provide assistance to families regardless of their faith and so would service Muslims, Christians, and Yazidis alike. The concept was based upon a program that had been run earlier in the ISIS war by the Archdiocese of Erbil on its own with great success and efficiency. The archdiocese had used funding that came completely from private, faith-based donors. In that project, total overhead expenses had been less than 5 percent.

In the present project, the proposed funding would be coming from USAID, and total overhead expense would be approximately 38 percent, with nearly $1 million of that to go directly to the US headquarters office of the NGO to cover their assigned portion of the overhead. While the archdiocese would have gladly run the project on its own, thus either increasing substantially the funds available for the displaced families, or decreasing substantially the cost to the US taxpayers who were ultimately funding the program, the archdiocese would not have then qualified as an entity under the long-established USAID funding requirements. In other words, the Church, on its own, did not meet the USAID administrative process requirements to run a program which it had demonstrably been running successfully on its own for over four years. The established NGO did have the ability to meet the administrative process requirements, but in doing so, would add nearly $2 million to the overall cost. The cost difference here was due entirely to administrative and compliance costs imposed by US funding requirements, none of which had any substantive impact on the quantity or quality of service being provided.[7]

While this project was in its preliminary application stages, Pope Francis addressed a gathering in Rome of Catholic charities from around the world. In a report published in the online *Crux Magazine*, Francis

---

[7] In a clear acknowledgement of the problem of excessive overhead and inefficiency in government aid funding, USAID under Administrator Mark Green initiated the New Partners Initiative in 2019 which sought to provide funding and capacity building assistance directly to local organizations in the target countries. In October, 2019, the Catholic University of Erbil, founded by Archbishop Bashar Warda in 2014, became one of the first recipients of funding under this program.

said, "Let us ask the Lord for him to free us of efficiency-ism, of world-liness, of the subtle temptation to worship ourselves and our abilities." He urged those before him to remember, "People before programs!"[8] And yet, in the multi-billion-dollar industry of international aid, the program, or process, has become everything.

In Iraq, we saw this most commonly in well-funded programs from established NGOs that spoke the requisite aid-speak in their appli-cations and proposals. Millions of dollars were made available for programs that would concentrate on "building bridges between com-munities" and "developing concentric layers of trust" for implementing "cross cultural reconciliation" and so on. We were looking for food, shelter, medicine, and security. As for reconciliation, the Christians would forgive, but further than that, they were unwilling to go. For the Christians, reconciliation required a fundamental change in mentality and ideology in those that had supported and participated in the per-secution and violence against the minorities, preceded by some form of public acceptance of responsibility. When these issues had been dealt with, reconciliation might be a discussion. But until then, such programs were not worth the time it took to explain them. For the Christians and Yazidis, they had been sitting in their homes and people had tried to come and kill them, while their neighbors stood by and encouraged it all. To the extent they could understand these "reconcilia-tion" and "bridge building" programs, they were incredulous that people could even propose such things. What world did they live in?

If there is one element of hope as it pertains to the global aid paradigm, out of all the hardship and tragedy that surrounds the displacement of the Christians in Iraq, it is the realization that without training, cre-dentials, established processes, or programs, a handful of priests, sisters, and laypeople took care of over 100,000 homeless people for over two years on private funding for a fraction of the cost of similar institutional aid programs. In doing so, they delivered services at a level which even the UN admitted they could not meet. There is an important lesson in this comparison for policy makers, for taxpayers, and most importantly,

---

8 Ines San Martin, "Pope warns charity leaders to steer clear of 'efficiency-ism'," *Crux*, May 24, 2019, accessed October, 2019, https://cruxnow.com/vatican/2019/05/24/pope-warns-charity-leaders-to-steer-clear-of-efficiency-ism.

for the people at-risk themselves. For a pittance, an objective analysis could be done as to why this difference in overhead expense exists and what the contributing factors are behind its continued existence.

There is an Aid Industrial Complex in our current world. Its impact on aid policy and implementation is overwhelming, and it is the poor and the needy who suffer the most from it. In my nearly five years in Iraq, I met no one who denied the deep problems within the international aid system, not even those who were part of it.

* * *

THIS BOOK IS MEANT TO SHOW what the situation has been and still is for the remaining Christians of Iraq and, in a more anecdotal sense, for the Christians of the Middle East. Admittedly, much of the story has been grim. Even when all of the false starts, failed promises, and missed opportunities are weighed in, it may be that the arc of history has just come too far to be overcome in any stabilization or restoration program, regardless of how well-intentioned they may be. The steady stream of violence from within broad sectors of Islam, pitting Muslim against Muslim, and Islam against the world, may simply need to play itself out in much the same way that Christians went through their centuries of slaughter and mayhem against each other in the not too distant past.[9] There is a point at which the reality of a thing becomes undeniable and unavoidable. There is no easy peace on the horizon in the Middle East, and no thinking person there believes that there is not still a long time of bloodshed ahead.

And yet not all is completely lost for the Christians of Iraq. To begin with, as a point of fundamental truth in the Christian experience, the example of the persecuted Christian is hardly new. I recall the comment of an aging Jesuit father in Washington, DC, when speaking about the dwindling numbers of Christians left in Iraq. "Well," he said, "remember. Christ only had twelve. And everybody wanted to kill them too."

Certainly, such Christians that choose to stay in Iraq will need courage and endurance to rival that of the apostles, which first brought

---

9 For a depiction of faith-driven Christian on Christian atrocities see *Les Grandes Miseres de la Guerre*, a set of 18 etchings by the French Artist Jaques Callot first published in 1633 showing in detail the horrors of the 30 years war (1592-1635).

Christianity to their land nearly two thousand years ago. But that spirit exists, and in many ways it appears now that in the horrors of the past decades, a scourging and tempering has honed the remaining Christians to the strength and temper they will need going forward.

Examples within the Church and elsewhere are not hard to find. In the examples of Fr. Thabet, Fr. Salar, Fr. Aram, Fr. Emmanuel, and Fr. Georges we find men who continue to deal with daily disappointment and danger and yet have not wavered for their people when crisis was at hand. The efforts of the deacon, now Fr. Shwan, were worth any of the next hundred people you could find.

We see examples as well in Archbishop Najeeb Michael, the former Dominican priest who risked his life to preserve the ancient Christian and Islamic manuscripts of Mosul and Baghdede. He crammed his car full of boxes and binders as ISIS fighters shot their way into the town, then patiently, diligently worked to preserve it all in makeshift storage spaces throughout the displacement. He recently accepted the newly-reinstalled role of archbishop of Mosul, dedicating his life now to restoring and preserving a Christian presence in that hostile city where so many of his predecessors were murdered before.

We see it in Archbishop Bashar Warda of Erbil, not content to simply survive, but incessantly encouraging and demanding of his people that they work to thrive and to show their legitimate place and full value to the plurality of Iraq. This attitude is expressed in his founding of his two anchor institutions: the Catholic University of Erbil—opened in the midst of the ISIS war—and the recently opened Maryamana Hospital in Ankawa, run by the Archdiocese of Erbil but open to the needy of all faiths. In both instances, the archbishop is building on the long history in the Middle East and elsewhere of providing Christian witness to the world through education and medical care.

We see it in Archbishop Habib of Basra, laboring away in his small and beleaguered diocese, looking for inspiration to the example of Mother Theresa, providing a Christian witness of service and hope while surrounded by grinding poverty and hostility on every side.

We see it in the Patriarch Cardinal Louis Sako, courageously making a stand for his people in Baghdad and throughout Iraq, insisting through his voice that the Christians of Iraq not be marginalized and deprived

An Iraqi Christian soldier stands guard outside Mass in Karemlesh, Nineveh Plain, Northern Iraq, June 2017. Inside His Beatitude, Patriarch Louis Sako and Fr. Thabet Habib consoled and encouraged patience for the citizens of Karemlesh who had traveled out to the still empty town for the day to show their resolve to return. Just five weeks later, the Knights of Columbus would announce a USD $2 million grant to rebuild the town, spurring a return of the people that allowed recovery to begin.

of their legitimate and necessary place in the historical weave of that ancient land. I will forever remember the blazing June day in 2017 when I stood at the back of the congregation as the Patriarch celebrated Mass for the distraught, still displaced citizens of Karamlesh in their shattered town. It had yet to even receive restored power or water, but the people had traveled back there for the day to show their intent to return. Making clear his solidarity with his people, the Patriarch stayed for hours afterward in the sweltering heat to patiently answer questions and give his people hope for return, while armed Christian security forces stood outside the heavily-damaged church, ever vigilant for the remnant ISIS fighters still roaming the greater Mosul region.

We see it as well in the dedicated laypeople who have willingly chosen to stay in Iraq, come what may, many of whom have found in their persecution a much deeper connection with their faith and its central story. And while the overall population continues to be driven down, and as the reality of return to much of Nineveh fades away, this seemingly permanent and small core continues to coalesce in the enclave of Ankawa. Still stubbornly in Baghdad. In Al-Qosh, which looked down from its mountainside home over the Nineveh Plain in defiance to ISIS throughout the war, a deep spirituality remains in its ancient streets, its churches and high above, the monastery of Mar Hormizd.

The history and teachings of Christianity requires of its adherents that they take the long view, plant the seed, and have faith that it will grow. In the land that witnessed both the Crucifixion and the resurrection of Jesus Christ, that is the best that the Christians of Iraq and the Middle East can do now. The history of the coming fifty years will tell the rest.

And not only in this way, but we boast also in afflictions, for we know that affliction perfects patience in us, And patience, experience, and experience, hope, But hope does not disappoint, because the love of God has come in, overflowing our hearts by The Spirit of Holiness who has been given to us.

ROMANS 5:3-5
(Translation from the Aramaic Bible)

Postscript

In the genocide years of the ISIS war and its aftermath, two diverging paths remained for the Christians of Iraq. In the first, they would be relegated to a vanishing community on their way to an inevitable end, their ancient presence dwindling down to that of a caretaker church of a museum people. In the second, they had been honed down to a resilient few, small in number yet tested and tempered in their faith and character, from which a resurrection could begin. For much of the time during which this book was written, it seemed the former would inexorably, tragically be the path of the Christians of Iraq. And yet, distant signs remained that the other path, more hopeful if also far more difficult and dangerous, might still lie ahead.

But there had been no expectation of the astounding flood of hope which burst forth out of the mass protests that spread from Baghdad and throughout much of Iraq beginning in October 2019. In a movement which was, in the main, unforeseen by sophisticated analysts (once again) ordinary Shia Muslims in the south of Iraq took to the streets by the millions, most of them young, unemployed, and suffering relentlessly under the grinding, grotesque corruption of the ruling power factions which had held revolving authority since the US invasion in 2003. Meanwhile, major western media outlets, apparently numb to news of further upheaval and chaos in Iraq on the one hand and without resources as to stories which required presence and hard journalistic diligence on the other, largely missed the enormity of what was transpiring.

His Beatitude, Patriarch Cardinal Louis Sako (center) surrounded by the bishops of Baghdad, travels on foot to Tahrir Square on November, 2, 2019, in a dramatic show of Christian solidarity with the mainly Shia anti-government protestors. Their arrival and presence met with an overwhelming welcome from Muslims and Christians alike.

In a complete repudiation of the constitution and government structure which had been left behind in Iraq by the Bush and Obama administrations, the young, increasingly secular, Shia demonstrators demanded a removal of the Islamic religious establishment from interference in politics, an abolition of sectarian quotas, the disbanding of all militias, and the drafting of a new constitution which enshrined these goals. In their purpose, the demands were a clear statement that the majority of the Shia people of Iraq had had enough with the involvement of religious and sectarian power factions, and with outside influences (mainly Iranian) in Iraqi governance and security. In effect, the protestors, mostly Shia Muslims themselves, were demanding an end to political Islam, and an end to the *Hashd* militias along with the competing, corrupt, sectarian factions which had given rise to them.

In all of this chaos, an opening of astonishing hope presented itself for the Christians who watched cautiously at first. Then, as the protest swelled throughout the country and its meaning became clear, the Christians joined fully in the demonstrations themselves, declaring openly both their Iraqi-Christian identity and their support for a new Iraq in which the ousting of the existing Islamic-based power factions might also finally, almost miraculously, provide a real place of inclusion and freedom for the Christians as full Iraqi citizens, a place that they had been so brutally denied throughout most of their history and most glaringly in the prior fifteen years. In a clear indication of the newly born solidarity which had seemingly arrived, Iraqi social media, Christian and Muslim alike, erupted in approval on November 2 when His Beatitude Cardinal Louis Sako, together with the assembled bishops of Baghdad, walked in unison to Tahrir Square to deliver medicine and comfort to the protestors.

But while the protestors in Iraq maintained a peaceful if overwhelming presence throughout October and into November, the Iranian theocracy, and the power factions they had built and supported in Iraq, sensed the mortal danger to their control and fought back with the tools they knew best: violence, intimidation, and intrigue, this last effort mostly in the form of tired attempts at deflection of responsibility towards alleged Israeli and American plots. Yet on the streets, the masses of people were having none of it. By early November, widely circulated videos from the center of the protest in Baghdad's Tahrir Square showed banners with the images of Grand Ayatollah Khamenei, the Supreme Leader of Iran, and Qasem Soleimani, leader of the Iranian Al Quds force, being beaten with shoes and defaced by angry Iraqi Shia demonstrators. Soleimani had been a continuing presence in Iraq for over a decade as the key enforcer in Iranian designs to control the military power of the country while Khamenei had until then been viewed as the untouchable Shia overlord of Iranian influence within Iraq. For the young Iraqi Shias, however, this Iranian-orchestrated power structure had brought them nothing but corruption, destruction, and despair. They wanted a future, and they wanted their country, and increasingly they saw Iranian intrusion as depriving them of both.

In the looming showdown that still lay ahead, violence, suppression and tragic disappointment were certainly foreseeable outcomes. Non-Shia power blocs, namely the minority Kurdish and Sunni, hedged on their involvement, deeply concerned about what any change might mean for them. And yet in the minds of the millions of protesting Shia, now joined fully by the remaining Christians, a future of hope was equally possible, however fraught with danger that path might be. For the Christians, that path was nothing short of liberation, and to them,

Photo courtesy of Chaldean Archdiocese of Baghdad

Iraqi Christian joining with Shia Muslim protestors, Baghdad, October 2019, with a Christian school in background. The emblem on his shirt is the Arabic "N" or Nun—the same symbol which ISIS sympathizers painted on the doors of Christian homes in Iraq to identify them as Nazarenes, or Christians, during the ISIS genocide against Christians of 2014. Draped around his shoulders is the Iraqi national flag.

the danger now meant nothing. This time they would be standing openly and together with their Iraqi brothers and sisters, no longer afraid of showing their Christian identities and instead, publicly affirming their role and place as equal and willing citizens of their own country in its time of crisis. And if their country would once again be forced down further into the abyss, at least now the Christians sensed they would not go down alone, but together with all those in Iraq who fought for hope, a fight in which the equal and welcomed participation of the Christians was in itself a miracle which few would ever have believed possible just months before. Regardless of what the coming weeks and months might hold, in finally reaching common cause with their protesting Muslim brothers and sisters, however briefly it might eventually prove to be, a seed of reconciliation had been planted.

In the Christian story all does not end at Golgotha, the bleak hill of Christ's Crucifixion. For the hopeful Christians of Iraq who joined with the marching millions of Baghdad in the autumn and winter of 2019, their own resurrection story awaits.

Acknowledgments

This book would still be an idea without the encouragement of George Russell, who thought this story needed be told and who guided me into the world of publishers. I am grateful to my agent, Lynne Rabinoff, and the team at Post Hill Press, whose patience and support allowed flexibility for the realities under which the book was written.

In the world of private aid providers, I thank my friends at the Knights of Columbus and Aid to the Church in Need, without whom the story of this book would have been drastically more tragic. To those at the Nazarene Fund, I will forever be thankful for you being open and listening to us when it counted most. To all of you, lives have been saved and futures preserved because of your work and charity.

Within the Catholic Church, I thank all those in the US, UK, Slovakia, Hungary, Belgium, and elsewhere who took me in as a brother during my travels. In the US, I particularly thank the Sisters of the Little Workers of the Sacred Heart in Washington, DC, who supported and protected me from the very beginning. I also thank the Franciscans of the monastery in Kennebunkport, Maine, whose constant presence has provided to me and to so many others a welcoming space for contemplation and renewal. In Iraq, I thank all the bishops, priests, deacons, sisters, and lay people who have been as family to me these past five years. You are all what I think of as what still stands as the truly good and necessary mission for the Church in these troubled times.

I give special thanks to David Trimble, Kent Hill, Andrew Walther, Nathaniel Hurd, Jeremy Barker, and Nina Shea, whose regular advice, wisdom, and friendship kept me going. I also thank Alexander D., Larry

V., Mike D. and Mike S., who did not abandon me when, through this work, I seemingly abandoned them at least for a time. I extend thanks as well to my lawyer Stephen Roberts, who listened and helped me manage my way through the complexities of this work.

For many reasons, in most cases due to safety or confidentiality, the nature of this book does not allow to me to acknowledge by name all those others who made it possible. I will trust and pray that they all know who they are. I make special note here of the many people within the US and other governments, and also the UN, who continue to do their best to make positive changes where they can, many of whom have been of immeasurable help in the writing of this book and the efforts it describes.

Lastly, this book, and all the work and struggle behind it, would not have been possible without my family and their patience and constant support. Included here are both my parents, now deceased, and my ancestors before them, who planted the seed for this work in me.